THE
UNSUSPECTED
POWER
OF THE PSALMS

THE UNSUSPECTED POWER OF THE PSALMS

Thomas R. Hawkins

THE UPPER ROOM

Nashville, Tennessee

To

ARTHUR LEE WISEMAN

Blessed are those who care for the poor and the weak.
Yahweh will save them in time of trouble.
Yahweh will protect them and give them life,
making them secure in the land.

—Psalm 41:1–2a, AP

CONTENTS

Introduction   9

1. Finding the Lost Spoor of Meaning   13
2. Disclosing the Heart and Mind of Jesus   22
3. Seeing New Patterns in Old Designs   39
4. Cracking Open the Hardened Shell   56
5. Hearing the Echo of a Forgotten Voice   68
6. Giving Shape to Formless Yearnings   81
7. Unlocking the Storehouse of Forgotten Possibilities   89
8. Rediscovering an Unsuspected Power   103

Appendix 1
    Organization of the Psalter   118
Appendix 2
    Form for Morning and Evening Prayer   121
Notes   124

INTRODUCTION

WHY THE PSALMS?

Often the dullest moment on Sunday morning is when the liturgist says, "Now turn with me to the back of the hymnal and join with me in reciting responsive reading...." The mechanical and montonous readings of the psalms that are found in hymnals can be not only singsong in character, but also devoid of meaning. For many Christians whose only exposure to the Psalter is a hymnal, these poems and hymns represent one of the least interesting and most unfamiliar portions of scripture.

The wide range of human emotion expressed in the psalms presents another problem for some Christians. We have been raised in an atmosphere where "church people" simply do not express themselves in ways that are not "nice," at least not in church. The psalms, with their thirst for vengeance and angry vindictiveness, are far too raw and blunt. We might want to grind our teeth and mutter all manner of ill under our breath at a church meeting. We might even want to bluster and fume about it once we get home. But we are reluctant to risk saying directly what we feel. The raw emotion found in the Psalter disturbs us and makes us uncomfortable.

We are often at a loss to understand why past generations found so much comfort and strength in the psalms and why they recommended them so highly. Surely they must have seen something we are overlooking. "All scripture is inspired by God and profitable for teaching," Paul admonishes us in Second Timothy 3:16 (RSV). But even the psalms? One can only wonder.

What, then, are we to make of these strange and disturbing writings? My journey with the psalms first began some years ago. St. Mark's Episcopal Church of

Westford, Massachusetts, invited me to conduct a Lenten study on the psalms. The Psalter plays an important role in Episcopal Sunday worship and in the offices of morning and evening prayer, and they wanted help in understanding this important worship resource.

What I offered to them was a short course in modern scholarship related to the psalms. I explained the various poetic forms found in the psalms. I drew their attention to the similarity of the psalms to other literature in the ancient Near East. I discussed divine kingship in Sumer and Egypt as it related to the royal psalms. I presented what we know of the Babylonian New Year Festival and how the psalms of enthronement might reflect this background. I shared what I knew of the psalms as they related to this scholar's reconstructed Covenant Renewal Festival or that scholar's New Year Festival.

The people at Saint Mark's were very polite. They listened attentively. They discussed intelligently. But I left the experience vaguely troubled. I felt that I had helped them understand the psalms as a poetic form, but I had not helped connect them to the psalms as a resource in their own spiritual lives. I had not enabled them to allow the psalms to enrich their understanding of what it meant to be Christian.

Some months later, a second disturbing note was struck. I was attending a discussion between Christians and Jews in which we were sharing our respective faiths and attempting to come to a deeper appreciation for and understanding of our different religious paths. The topic was "grace." One Jewish participant had attempted to connect the Jewish notion of God's *chesed* with Christian grace. *Chesed* is a word that occurs frequently in the psalms, where it is usually translated as "steadfast love" or "lovingkindness." This analysis provoked a strong reaction from many of the Jewish participants. They stated over and over again that *grace* was not a word they had heard while growing up in a Jewish household. The psalms, they stressed, were not part of the mainstream of Jewish thought.

Once again I was thrown back to the psalms. Even though I did not fully appreciate the psalms, I sensed that they were indeed within the mainstream of Christian thought. Why does the language of *The Book of Common Prayer* echo so much of the Psalter? Why does the monastic daily office prescribe such massive doses from the Psalter? Why, when just the New Testament is published, are the psalms often appended to the same volume? How much, I wondered, is our Christian understanding of grace and of our whole faith mediated through the metaphors and images of the psalms? It was not until much later that, almost by accident, I returned to the psalms both intentionally and intensively.

The following pages are the fruit of my reflections upon the psalms. While I have firmly set them within what some theologians would call a "Christocentric" reading, I do want to affirm that I fully understand and accept the essential Jewishness of the Psalter. I trust I have not erred in a too radical Christocentrism. I am simply trying to explore what the psalms have meant to me, as a Christian, as I have read them on a daily basis over a considerable period of time.

I have come to believe that the psalms are an incredibly rich resource for the contemporary church. Stirrings within the church indicate that I am not the only person to be reaching this conclusion. New translations are appearing. New musical settings for the Psalter are being composed. Those responsible for the revision of approved liturgies within several denominations are advocating the restoration of the psalms to Sunday worship.

More and more people within the church are simultaneously struggling to recover some disciplined life of prayer and service within their lives. This renewal of spirituality, I feel, can be nurtured and sustained by a recovery of the Psalter within our private worship as well as our public praise of God. The psalms are an important resource in learning once again how to pray. The psalms yield their riches only to those willing to pray them faithfully and regularly.

This study is intended to support and to enhance the ongoing recovery of the psalms within both the public and private worship of God. Questions for reflection have been included at the end of each chapter which may be used for individual or group study. I have learned some things since that Lent at Saint Mark's, and I have not dealt with the many scholarly issues surrounding the psalms. However, a brief summary of the Psalter's organization has been included as an appendix, as well as a form for using the psalms in morning and evening prayer.

The psalms truly are a grammar of praise that teach us a way of prayer. Just as my life has been touched by daily companionship with the Psalter, so I hope that through this study others may gain a new appreciation for the Psalter as a resource in their own personal spiritual life and in their corporate worship as the Household of God.

CHAPTER ONE: *Finding the Lost Spoor of Meaning*

DURING THE COLD months of January and February the surface waters of the stormy North Atlantic Ocean grow increasingly chilly as the water absorbs the cold temperature of the winds that gust above it. These cold and heavy waters gradually begin to sink, slipping down and displacing the warmer layers below them. Rich stores of minerals, some derived from abandoned shells of diatoms, some the decayed compost of dead sea creatures, some the rich minerals swept off the continents by the action of rain and wind, are churned upward. These nutrients rise to the surface and kindle the flame of spring in the thin dusting of life that has slept upon the waters during the long winter.

I suspect that a similar process occurs within our own lives. The surface levels of our consciousness float along, preoccupied with superficial matters. Then, as our attention focuses upon a particular problem or perplexity, the weight of that thought glides downward to the warmer and more hidden levels of our being. It displaces some ancient richness of experience or some long-forgotten memory that then rises upward to illuminate and renew our lives.

Laurens Van Der Post in *The Lost World of the Kalahari* tells how his parents told him stories of the long-vanished South African Bushmen during his childhood. When he became an adult, struggling to understand what was happening to his life and to his nation, those childhood memories returned to haunt him. Eventually they drove him to undertake a difficult and dangerous journey into the Kalahari Desert in search of the lost race of African Bushmen. This external journey is paralleled by a personal journey across an inner wilderness just as complex and as perilous as the desert. Reflecting upon his memories, Van Der Post writes:

> One of the most moving aspects of life is how long the deepest memories stay with us. It is as if individual memory is enclosed in a greater, which even in the night of our forgetfulness stands like an angel with folded wings ready, at the moment of acknowledged need, to guide us back to the lost spoor of our meanings.[1]

On a safari the hunter carefully watches for the *spoor*, the tracks left by wild game in the soil. Only the spoor can lead the hunter to the place of encounter with the beast that the hunter is pursuing. We all seek to rediscover the lost spoor of our meanings, Van Der Post implies. Our hearts and spirits are powerful tools in our pursuit of encounter with the divine and the demonic within us.

Such a lost spoor was recently churned up within me. As a boy I had to hurry home from school to help with evening chores on our family farm. One chore was to go through the feed lots and check the water fountains scattered throughout them. I had to dig the mud out of the fountain with my hand so that it would not stop up the water float. Then I had to check the water level in the tanks. Usually that meant that the hose had to be rolled out to the tank and the tank filled. One such fountain was an old fifty-gallon oil drum, turned on its side and resting on a sled of osage orange fence posts. A square hole had been cut in the top of the drum to use when filling the tank. Since the hogs could not be trusted to leave the hose alone, I had to stand or sit there and watch the tank until it was full. It always filled slowly. I can remember one crisp autumn afternoon I came home and started to fill that oil drum with water. The Gideons had visited my school that day and had distributed small New Testaments with the Book of Psalms. It was palm-sized and had a maroon cover. I had never owned a Bible. My parents did not attend a church. I remember sitting atop that oil drum, legs astraddle it, reading Psalm 1. I suspect that the memory impressed itself upon me because of the relationship between the water gushing

out of the hose into the hog fountain and the images in
Psalm 1:

> They are like a tree that is planted
> by water streams,
> yielding its fruit in season,
> its leaves never fading;
> success attends all they do.
> —Psalm 1:3, AP

The words made absolutely no sense to me. I can sense
the perplexity even now. Everyone, especially my sixth-
grade teacher and the Gideon visitors, had told me that
the Bible was a book that I should read and that was
terribly important to my life. But I could not decipher the
clues hidden beneath the strong cadences of Elizabethan
poetry. I stuck the maroon book in my hip pocket and
later tossed it onto the upper shelf of my closet. I found it
years later when, after my father died, we moved to
another house. That is my only childhood memory of the
psalms. Indeed, it is my only childhood memory of
anything related to the Bible.

I did not pick up another Bible until I was in college.
By then I was feeling my way into the Christian community.
I purchased my own copy of the newly-published *New
English Bible* from a bookstore in Paris, Illinois. The deciding
factor was that this edition was printed in lines that ran
across the page rather than in columns, as that perplexing
maroon pocket version had had. I was determined to
read this one cover to cover. Even the genealogies did not
deter me. I marched along until I reached the psalms.
Once again I found them inaccessible. I found no entry
point for connecting my own emotions and thoughts to
them. The language seemed unrealistic. I could not
understand the emotions. I was mystified at the suggestion
that these writings had such a hold on generations of
men and women. They seemed repetitive, always saying
the same thing over and over again, in almost the same
words. Even that one thing, whatever it was, did not
seem obvious or important to me. I could not perceive
the lesson I believed I ought to find somewhere in them.

By the time I finished scanning them (I had to lumber through them before I could go on to the next book in any case), I had developed a violent mental block against reading the psalms. It has taken many years and much study to dissolve that block.

I share all this because I think that it illustrates the fact that we cannot really "read" the psalms with meaning until we have lived through some of life's tragic and exhilarating hours. Once we reach the midpoint of life, the reality of our mortality strikes home. A parent has perhaps died. Ambitions have been tempered by reality. Physical strength is no longer growing. We understand the frailties of human flesh and the fragility of human feeling. I could not understand the psalms as a child and as a teenager because I had not yet lived enough. I did not understand what it meant to be divided against myself. I had not experienced the push-and-pull of wanting to be loved, but fearing love. I had not dreamed boldly enough to see those dreams shattered by forces beyond me.

Until we have felt deep within us the pulses of our own souls, the psalms remain only words on a page. Until we are willing to sense and to accept our own inner emotions in all their positive and negative moments, the psalms will remain flat and inaccessible. Beautiful perhaps. Saturated with childhood memories of a grandparent reading to us the psalm of the good shepherd. Laden with the warmth of some well-loved Sunday school teacher. But flat. The existential power of the psalms is released only when we are able to bring the fullness of our emotional life to them. For those whose memory of the psalms is freighted with such good and happy childhood recollections, so unlike my own, I suggest that these very sentimental memories form another kind of block to entering into the psalms. The psalms do not deal in sentiment. They commerce in raw emotion. Our pleasant childhood memories block our passage into the Psalter's deeper levels of feeling. Our surface memories block our discovery of the lost spoor of a more intense and cosmic memory that encompasses us and discloses itself to us in the psalms. If we are graced, then we will discover that the psalms reveal the spoor, or tracks, of our own journey. We will realize that their words trace the form and the shape of the unspoken and conflicting yearnings within us, which are our dubious consequence of having been created a little less than the angels, yet crowned with glory.

The psalms give speech to the muzzled voices of anguish and praise, of sorrow and confidence, of will and purpose within us. We desperately need to recover such speech. The disenchantment of the world that has been one result of modern scientific culture has left individuals without validation for their inner lives. This disenchantment transforms what was previously only a means into an end of human activity. The specialization and institutionalization of modern life have turned us into "specialists without spirit, sensualists without heart," as Max Weber once wrote.[2] We are trapped in an iron cage of our own making.

Indeed, it was this realization that drove me back to the psalms and their strange world of meaning. I had spent several days in Berlin. One day I passed via U-bahn into East Berlin. I walked along Unter den Linden and windowshopped on drab streets. I sauntered through Alexander Platz and sat quietly in the thirteenth-century Marienkirche, Berlin's oldest remaining church. Everywhere I was struck by the drabness of life. Even the ice cream I ordered in a sidewalk cafe seemed tasteless and colorless, floating without substantial form in its stark metal dish.

In sharp contrast to this was West Berlin. Neon lights and gaudy display windows hawked their wares to passersby along Kurfürstendamm. I was not sure which was worse: the gaudy but hollow appearance of Kurfürstendamm or the bleak emptiness of Unter den Linden. Although the people lived under two radically different social systems, they seemed equally trapped in Weber's iron cage and were either specialists without spirit or sensualists without heart. They embodied two contrary impulses I had felt stirring within me. I suddenly recognized that they both stemmed from a far more profound dis-ease.

All of us have become tools of our tools, of our ideas

and concepts, of our machines. Our inner being has been muffled. We have been left unable to hear or to see. We have grown alienated from ourselves, as more of our inner and outer lives are turned over to unseen, inexplicable forces. That, after all, may be the most disquieting aspect of the computer revolution. Electronic and computer developments distance us increasingly from understanding. As a child, I could pry the back off of my wristwatch and, looking inside for a few minutes, discover how it worked. Peering at my digital clock, I can learn nothing and understand even less. All this breeds what some have called a "black box" mentality. We passively accept that more and more of life will be controlled by little black boxes whose mysterious workings we cannot comprehend.

As I sat in Alexander Platz that afternoon eating my ice cream, all these reflections came together with another set of recent experiences. A few weeks earlier I had spent several days in a religious community whose common life was structured around a modified daily office. Four times each day the community gathered to pray and to hear the reading of scripture. The psalms provided the main vehicle for expression of feeling and for congregational participation in these offices. I had reacted strongly against the predominate part being played by the psalms. My past experience caused me to respond negatively. The extensive use of psalms, no matter how sensitively done, made it difficult for me to enter fully into the experience of common prayer. As the days passed, however, I discovered that something important was happening to me. Emotions and feelings deep within me were being evoked by these psalms, though I could not identify how or why.

Sitting in that sidewalk cafe, I suddenly recognized that the psalms were a puzzle to me because I had allowed most of my personal life as well as the greater world around me to become a puzzle. I also realized that for me the psalms had not only diagnosed the problem but also provided a solution as well. The psalms open our inner ears and eyes by first opening our outer voices. Their passion for all of life rouses from its slumber our own drugged and alienated inmost being. To pray the psalms is to pray with the heart. The psalms stir something deep within us and bring it into the fertile reaches of our lives. They teach us a grammar of praise, which we have forgotten how to articulate. The psalms lead us along the path of forgotten treasures and urge us forward into a new future.

In that palm-sized Gideon New Testament that I had been given in the sixth grade, the psalms were appended to the books of the New Testament. For years I had been puzzled by this fact. I had never been able to discover why, of all the books in the Hebrew Bible, the psalms merited this honor. I am puzzled no longer. In the New Testament we find a variety of accounts that bear witness to a new mode of being-in-the-world that is revealed in Jesus, the Christ. These narratives are accounts external to the main character. They provide a rich resource for what others around Jesus thought significant and meaningful about him. These eyewitnesses have left us stories about Jesus' healings and controversies, about his sayings and parables. Occasionally there is a brief flash of insight into Jesus' inner life. He wept for his friend Lazarus. He was so overcome with fear that the sweat poured off him like great drops of blood. In anger he cursed the fig tree or overturned the tables in the Temple. For the most part, however, the New Testament provides no sustained access to Jesus' inner life.

The psalms, on the other hand, give us such entrance into Jesus' own spiritual life. This is how the church from its inception onward has always understood the psalms and why it has appended them so frequently to its New Testament. Understood as the prayers of Jesus, the psalms allow us to experience Jesus' emotional life as he expressed it through these prayers, laments, hymns, and thanksgivings. Jesus chose to pour his own feelings and spiritual struggles into the language of the Psalter as he prayed to his divine Parent. In turning to the psalms, then, we turn to Jesus' own prayerbook and find within it the traces of his own inner self.

But the psalms provide us with something more precious still. In his letter to the church at Philippi, Paul urges his hearers to "have this mind among yourselves, which is yours in Christ Jesus" (Phil. 2:5, RSV). Over and over again Paul stresses that the purpose of the Christian journey is to have that mind in us that was in Christ Jesus. We are to be conformed to Christ's image and being.

> I have been crucified with Christ; it is no longer I who live, but Christ who lives in me; and the life I now live in the flesh I live by faith in the Son of God, who loved me and gave himself for me.
>
> —Galatians 2:20, RSV

The end point of our lives is to bear within us that mind of Christ and in so doing to attain our fullest humanity. We find that mind of Christ and bring it into ourselves through the praying of the psalms. They are the prayers of Jesus that disclose to us his own inner being. By making these prayers our own, we enter into the same world of meanings that shaped Jesus' self-understanding and has provided every Christian generation since Paul with a means of conformity to the mind of Christ.

Many contemporary Christians experience large stretches of the Psalter as barren and meaningless. They wonder how the psalms could ever have been as precious as they once seem to have been. To embrace and to struggle with this strange prayerbook may feel as if one were plunging into cold and heavy water in early spring; but that confrontation may drift down into our depths and stir upward long-forgotten riches.

Questions for Reflection/Discussion

1. Take a few moments in silence to reflect upon your relationship with the psalms. Bring to mind your earliest remembrance of them, then follow your experience with them to the present, marking significant high points and low points along the way.

2. In reflecting upon your experiences with the psalms, what would you say has been your biggest difficulty? Why do you think this is so?

3. Now consider an instance when your life connected with the psalms in a powerful way, a time when the Psalter came alive for you. It may have been a time of personal crisis when words of a psalm gave strength and encouragement, or a verse on a religious greeting card that came at a critical moment. Perhaps it centered around verses from the psalms in personal devotions, in a sermon, or in a hymn. In what way did the psalms touch your life deeply? In what way were you changed by the psalms?

4. Find the psalm that connected with your life in the Bible and take a few moments to read and reflect upon it prayerfully.

5. If you are part of a group, find a partner and share as much of your reflections on these questions as you are comfortable sharing with one another. If you are studying on your own, you may find it helpful to record your reflections in a journal.

CHAPTER TWO: *Disclosing the Heart and Mind of Jesus*

MORE THAN ANY other canonical source, Jesus turns to the Psalter to understand who he is and what is his mission in history. Jesus opens his heart to us in the psalms. Thus, they lay bare for us the inner thoughts and prayers of Jesus. They disclose his personal journey from the first stirrings of his sense of true identity as the unique bearer of God's word to his final loss of hope in the face of death.

Jesus himself must have meditated upon and pondered the psalms extensively. He uses Psalms 22 and 31 to express his agony at the cross. In his teaching and preaching he cites directly Psalms 110, 118, and 41. Many other parables and sayings echo the images and poetry of the psalms. What Jesus says about himself as the good shepherd must surely have been shaped by Psalm 23 as well as by the prophetic and apocalyptic traditions. As every faithful Jew, Jesus would have joined in singing the Hallel psalms in the passover celebrations. Jesus' sensitive identification with the language and symbols of the psalms allowed them to shape his identity and self-understanding. Out of this profound identification, Jesus applied the Psalter's traditional associations to himself in a new and unique way.

This process of actualizing the old cultic hymns and folk poetry of Israel in the life of one historical person had begun long before Jesus. Perhaps as early as the exile, scribes had pondered how the old religious hymns and cult songs could remain meaningful. The old context of the Temple was gone, and it had provided a center for their meaningfulness. Yet these psalms were part of the deposit of tradition through which God had communicated with Israel. How were they to remain vital and alive? The solution was to place them within a new context. David had played a central role in the establishment of the Temple and its services. He was remembered as a musician and as a poet. Only a small step was required in order for David's life to become the new context for these psalms. The most accessible qualities of David were selected. Certain psalms were provided with superscriptions linking the psalm to a specific incident in David's life. The incidents chosen as evoking these psalms were not royal occasions or representative of the royal office. "David is pictured simply as a man...who displays all the strengths and weaknesses of all human beings. He emerges as a person who experiences the full range of human emotions, from fear and despair to courage and love, from complaint and plea to praise and thanksgiving."[1] David still remains the one chosen by God for the sake of Israel, but the emphasis falls on the inner life of David. An access is given into his emotional life. One can perceive how David's faith relates to the subjective and experiential side of David's life. Some psalms are also attached to historical events. While one might expect that this would have the effect of tying the hymns to the ancient past, it has the opposite effect. They are contemporized and individualized for every generation of the suffering and persecuted, the perplexed and the joyful.

> The psalms are transmitted as the sacred psalms of David, but they testify to all the common troubles and joys of ordinary human life in which all persons participate. These psalms do not need to be cultically actualized to serve later generations. They are made immediately accessible to the faithful. Through the mouth of David, the man, they become a personal word from God in each individual situation.[2]

In another man, born of the house of David, the psalms take on yet another context, more profound and pregnant with meaning than the one ascribed to the psalms by the scribes in exile. For the Christian, the psalms reveal not just the inner feelings of the man David, but also those of the messiah, the Word through whom God has disclosed the divine nature and desire. In being prayed by Jesus, Israel's psalms, offered in the midst of history's ebb and flow, acquire a new and unique intensity for the Christian community. They take on a new dimension when they are experienced in the framework of Jesus' life, death, and resurrection. The process of finding meaning in the old cultic hymns and folk poetry may have begun long before Jesus; but the Christian church finds the culmination of this long process in him. The psalms lay open Christ's emotional life. They disclose how Jesus' self-understanding shaped what he did and said and was. In this disclosure they also unveil God's own yearning for and anguish toward God's creation.

When John baptizes him, Jesus is overwhelmed by the power of this experience of divine election and adoption. The Gospels describe poetically what Jesus experienced through the image of the dove. Jesus himself turns in this moment of decision to the psalms in order to express his feelings. He says that he hears the spirit speaking to him the words of a royal messianic psalm: "He said to me, 'You are my son, today I have begotten you'" (Psalm 2:7, RSV). Only the psalms could give voice and order to Jesus' surging inner emotions in this moment of dawning self-understanding.

Driven out into the wilderness, Jesus faces the inner demons that urge him to abuse his power and to abandon his newly-discovered true identity for a false self, based not on who he is but rather on what he can perform. Jesus gives shape to his experience and responds to it by means of the psalms that rehearse Israel's wilderness experience.

The psalms of salvation history, such as Psalm 78, Psalm 105 or Psalm 106, recounted Israel's failure to overcome its demons during the time of its wilderness testing. Israel was tempted to create an identity for itself out of its own actions rather than to rely in trust upon God's gracious goodness. Israel fails the test by seeking its own food and doubting God's trustworthiness.

They only sinned against him more than ever,
defying the Most High in the desert,
deliberately challenging God
by demanding their favorite food.

They blasphemed against God,
"Is it likely," they said, "that God
could give a banquet in the wilderness?

"Admittedly, when he struck the rock,
waters gushed, torrents streamed out,
but bread now, can he give us that,
can he provide meat for his people?"

Yahweh was enraged when he heard them,
a fire flared at Jacob,
the wrath attacked Israel
for having no faith in God,
no trust in his power to save.
—Psalm 78:17–22

These psalms become the means by which Jesus understands and responds to his own inner turmoil and temptation.

Thus when Jesus is tempted to make bread for himself by Satan, he refuses. He answers,

It is written, "Man shall not live by bread alone, but by every word that proceeds from the mouth of God."
—Matthew 4:4, RSV

Jesus overcomes the failure of trust, which the psalms of salvation history trace as the beginning of Israel's troubles. When Satan tempts him to work wonders, Jesus responds again in terms drawn from the psalms. Showing that even the devil can quote scripture, Satan cites the following:

He will put you in his angels' charge
to guard you wherever you go.
They will support you on their hands
in case you hurt your foot against a stone.
—Psalm 91:11–13

Jesus, however, understands that the psalmist is expressing confidence in God as a God who is trustworthy and sure. God's protection depends upon God alone. Our attitude is to be that of the psalmist: absolute trust. Therefore, Jesus refuses to jump from the Temple because he, like the faithful psalmist, will not put God to the test. He refuses to verify, to quantify, or to analyze the depths of God's love and, instead, simply trusts in faith. Whatever the real nature of the inner temptations Jesus faced in the wilderness, the fact remains that he expressed these struggles using the language and the imagery of the psalms. The psalms provided him with a flexible container into which he could pour his inner turmoil, examine it, and give it a formed response.

The psalms offered Jesus this same medium through which to understand his experience and his destiny during his entire ministry. In the Beatitudes, Jesus distills his pondering and praying the psalms. They gather up and restate Israel's praise of God out of the depths of abandonment and sorrow, of defeat and lonely exile, of return and revival. The Beatitudes echo the psalms' concern with the defeated and the sorrowing, with the poor and the abused, with all those who struggle to remain faithful to their vision in spite of life's complexities. In the process, they reveal, through the heart of Jesus, the immense pathos of God.

—Blessed are the poor in spirit.

He will free the poor man who calls to him,
    and those who need help,
he will have pity on the poor and feeble,
    and save the lives of those in need;
he will redeem their lives from exploitation and outrage,
    their lives will be precious in his sight.
                                        —Psalm 72:12–14a

—Blessed are those who mourn.

        "Hear, Yahweh, take pity on me;
        Yahweh, help me!"
    You have turned my mourning into dancing,

you have stripped off my sackcloth and wrapped me in
     gladness;
and now my heart, silent no longer, will play you music;
Yahweh, my God, I will praise you for ever.
                              —Psalm 30:10–12

—Blessed are the meek.

    A little longer, and the wicked will be no more,
    search his place well, he will not be there;
    but the humble shall have the land for their own
    to enjoy untroubled peace.
                              —Psalm 37:10–11

—Blessed are those who hunger and thirst for righteousness.

       Happy are we if we exercise justice
       and constantly practise virtue!
       Yahweh, remember me,
       for the love you bear your people,
       come to me as a savior,
       let me share the happiness of your chosen,
       the joys of your nation
       and take pride in being one of your heirs.
                              —Psalm 106:3–5

—Blessed are the merciful.

       Yahweh repays me as I act justly,
       as my purity is in his sight.
       Faithful you are with the faithful,
       blameless with the blameless,
       pure with the one who is pure,
       but crafty with the devious,
       you save a people that is humble
       and humiliate eyes that are haughty.
                              —Psalm 18:24–27

—Blessed are the pure in heart.

    Who has the right to climb the mountain of Yahweh,
    who has the right to stand in his holy place?
    He whose hands are clean, whose heart is pure,
    whose soul does not pay homage to worthless things
    and who never swears to a lie.

> The blessing of Yahweh is his,
> and vindication from God his savior.
> —Psalm 24:3–5

—Blessed are the peacemakers.

> Come, my sons, listen to me,
> I will teach you the fear of Yahweh.
> Which of you wants to live to the full,
> who loves long life and enjoyment of prosperity?
> Malice must be banished from your tongue,
> deceitful conversation from your lips;
> never yield to evil, practice good,
> seek peace, pursue it.
> —Psalm 34:11–14

Just as the Beatitudes' texture is in part defined by the psalms, so the texture and shape of Jesus' whole ministry is marked by the psalms. In praying the psalms, Jesus comes to image in his own life their universal dimension. When probed for why he speaks in parables, Jesus responds, "I will open my mouth in a parable; I will utter dark sayings from of old" (Psalm 78:2, RSV). Many parables center upon an image or metaphor drawn from the psalms. The parable of the rich fool who gathers his wealth but dies before he can enjoy it finds an echo in the equally pithy observations of Psalm 39:6. "Surely man goes about as a shadow! Surely for nought are they in turmoil; man heaps up, and knows not who will gather!" (RSV).

Having healed the centurion's paralyzed servant, Jesus alludes to Psalm 107:2–3. He proclaims that those who have faith such as this Gentile centurion will come from the East and the West to sit at table with Abraham while the children of this world will be thrown into the outer darkness.

> Give thanks to Yahweh, for he is good,
> his love is everlasting:
>
> let these be the words of Yahweh's redeemed,
> those he has redeemed from the oppressor's clutches,
> by bringing them home from foreign countries,
> from east and west, from north and south . . . .

> Pouring his contempt upon the nobly born,
> he left them to wander in a trackless waste.
>   —Psalm 107:1–3, 40

The shape of Jesus' language, the metaphors, the images, the stereotyped phrases reveal a personality steeped in the language of the psalms.

When the scribes and Pharisees contest his authority, Jesus turns to the psalms in order to vindicate himself. The psalms once again illuminate Jesus' self-understanding. When asked to identify himself, Jesus refers his accusers to the psalms. In particular, Jesus directs their attention to the royal psalms that speak of the messiah. If at an earlier stage in their development the scribes had poured the psalms into the personal history of David in order to ground them in the personal, subjective faith of a human person, Jesus boldly transfers this Davidic association to his own person. He quotes Psalm 82:6 as his defense when the Jews prepare to stone him to death for blasphemy.

> The Jews fetched stones to stone him, so Jesus said to them, "I have done many good works for you to see, works from my Father; for which of these are you stoning me?" The Jews answered him, "We are not stoning you for doing a good work but for blasphemy: you are only a man and you claim to be God." Jesus answered:
>
> "Is it not written in your Law:
> 'I said, you are gods?'
>
> So the Law uses the word gods
> of those to whom the word of God was addressed,
> and scripture cannot be rejected."
>   —John 10:31–35

Another time Jesus hurls at his accusers a defense based upon Psalm 110:1. He applies the Davidic authentication directly to himself, saying he is the "lord" that even David called "lord."

> He then said to them, "How can people maintain that the Christ is son of David? Why, David himself says in the Book of Psalms:

> " 'The Lord said to my Lord:
> Sit at my right hand
> and I will make your enemies
> a footstool for you.' "
> —Luke 20:41–43

Jesus' deepest point of identity with the psalms discloses itself in the relationship between the psalms of lament and the Passion. The entire sweep of Jesus' last days is given its fullest meaning when seen in the light of these psalms. As Jesus enters Jerusalem on Palm Sunday, the ancient cry of Psalm 118:26 is upon the people's lips. "Blessed be he who enters in the name of the Lord!" (RSV). When the scribes rebuke Jesus for allowing the crowds to honor him with these ancient words, Jesus responds by quoting back to his detractors the words of yet another psalm, Psalm 8:2: "By the mouth of babes and infants, thou hast founded a bulwark because of thy foes" (RSV).

The psalmist's words are on Jesus' lips while he hangs on the cross. He recites Psalm 22 because it alone can give voice to his utter sense of abandonment and defeat. It alone can vent his anger and express his unbroken trust in the One who is always faithful and might yet lift him from sterility and death. The whole warp and woof of the crucifixion finds itself woven into the language of Psalm 22.

> My God, my God, why have you deserted me?
> How far from saving me, the words I groan!
> I call all day, my God, but you never answer....
>
> Yet here am I, now more worm than man,
> scorn of mankind, jest of the people,
> all who see me jeer at me,
> they toss their heads and sneer,
> "He relied on Yahweh, let Yahweh save him!
> If Yahweh is his friend, let Him rescue him!"
>
> I can count every one of my bones,
> and there they glare at me, gloating;
> they divide my garments among them
> and cast lots for my clothes.
> —Psalm 22:1–2a, 6–8, 17–18

All the elements of the crucifixion are present. There are the smug plotters who have turned out to see the results of their work. The soldiers decide to cast lots for the clothes. Passersby shout and ask, "You saved others, can't you save yourself if you are the Son of God?" Even the centurion's acclamation, "Truly this was the Son of God," brings us back to the baptismal allusion of Psalm 2.

The imagery of the crucifixion also draws Psalm 69 into its orbit of meaning.

> It is for you I am putting up with insults
> that cover me with shame,
> that make me a stranger to my brothers,
> an alien to my mother's other sons;
> zeal for your house devours me,
> and the insults of those who insult you fall on
> me. . . .
>
> I found no one to console me.
> They gave me poison to eat instead,
> when I was thirsty they gave me vinegar to drink.
> —Psalm 69:7–9, 20c–21

Words from the Psalter that Jesus had prayed and sung so often throughout his life took on a new meaning in face of the cross. Jesus' experience of his passion is filtered and condensed, organized and given meaning, by his praying of the psalms.

If Psalm 69's allusion to a drink made of vinegar echoed in Jesus' heart as he hung on the cross, his voice recited Psalm 31. Jesus' last seven words include verses from this psalm as well as from Psalm 22. "Into thy hands I commit my spirit; thou hast redeemed me, O Lord, faithful God" (Psalm 31:5, RSV). While Psalm 31 begins as a powerful lament in the face of defeat and death, it ends with a lyric praise of a God who delivers the faithful and who acts dependably on behalf of those who place their trust in God:

> To every one of my oppressors
> I am contemptible,

loathsome to my neighbors,
    to my friends a thing of fear.

Those who see me in the street
    hurry past me;
I am forgotten, as good as dead in their hearts,
    something discarded.

I hear their endless slanders,
    threats from every quarter,
as they combine against me,
    plotting to take my life. . . .

Blessed be Yahweh, who performs
    marvels of love for me
    (in a fortress-city)!
In my alarm I exclaimed,
    "I have been snatched out of your sight!"
Yet you heard my petition
    when I called to you for help.
                    —Psalm 31:11–13, 21–22

The psalms of lamentation and complaint to God thus unveil Jesus' inner experiences and his personal faith's interaction with the complex, tumultuous world that confronted him.

The psalms of lament, of which Psalms 22 and 69 are a part, as prayers of Jesus remind us that Jesus' suffering and death gather into them not just sin and redemption, of which we in the church have made so much, but also Christ's healing and soothing of life's hurts by entering fully into our human wounds.

If, as in the New Testament, the work of Christ is described as salvation from sin and death, then (following the Old Testament understanding) by "death" we mean not only the cessation of life but the power of death at work within life which people experience in all types of suffering.[3]

Christ has descended into the pit of death and has submitted his own life to the powers that work against the fullness of life. From these depths he opens his inner life to us through the psalms of lament. Uniting his voice with the psalmist's voice, Christ has prayed and continually prays for us and with us in our own suffering. By joining our voices to theirs as we too pray the psalms, our suffering takes on new meaning.

These psalms often contain vicious and bitter maledictions, which the psalmist hurls at his or her enemies. These maledictions frequently offend the modern ear. Some versions of the Psalter omit them entirely, deeming them unsuitable for congregational use.

> Vent your fury on them,
> let your burning anger overtake them;
> may their camp be reduced to ruin,
> and their tents left unoccupied:
> for hounding a man after you had struck him,
> for adding more wounds to those which you inflicted.
>
> Charge them with crime after crime,
> deny them further access to your righteousness,
> blot them out of the book of life,
> strike them off the roll of the virtuous!
> —Psalm 69:24–28

Other psalms proclaim those blessed who dash their enemies' babies against the rock (Psalm 137:9). Yet even these were seen by the Christian community in a new light because Jesus had infused a new spirit into them through his own praying of them. The Hebrew word for vengeance that appears in these maledictions, *naqum*, is found in many covenants and treaties of the ancient Near East. It refers to the rightful power of the king or lord to enforce his codes and laws. Vengeance in these covenants is the king's exercise of his sovereign power to intervene and to protect his vassals when another hostile power threatens them. This power belongs only to the king. The vassal cannot exercise military force independently without breaking covenant.[4] Thus the psalmists affirm that "vengeance is the Lord's." Only God, as the sovereign lord standing in a covenant relationship to Israel, has the right and the duty to execute vindication. The harsh demands for God to intervene and execute vengeance are the urgent pleas of men and women who continue to trust in God when logic and self-interest should have driven them to take matters into their own hands. The maledictions are desperate cries from those who trust in the face of all temptation to rely on their own resources. They are affirmations of absolute obedience to God.

The true greatness of Jesus' life is found in his perfect conformity to this obedient trust. Like the psalmist, Jesus is obedient even unto death, death on a cross. This obedience sets him apart from others (John 5:30; 14:10; Matt. 26:42; Phil. 2:8). Others performed miraculous deeds. Others spoke eloquently of life and truth and beauty. The prophets criticized the hypocrisy of religious conformity. Many great thinkers, including Socrates, suffered cruel deaths as a witness to their ideals. Paul considered Jesus' obedience as the very source of our salvation (Rom. 5:19). To his last breath, Jesus demonstrates the utter obedience in the face of suffering that the psalms of lament portray. Like them, he pleads and cries out. Like them, he refuses to take matters into his own hands and act on his own behalf. He continues to trust in God's covenant loyalty. Vengeance belongs to the Lord; one must trust in God's vindication alone.

> His death by execution, which failed to shake his confidence in the coming rule of God, centred as it was in the interests of humanity—he continued, when faced with his approaching death, to proffer salvation on God's behalf—constitutes for us the challenging message that historical failures are not the last word—that even in radical fiascos we may continue to trust in God. . . . This life of Jesus calls us to a *metanoia*, to this effect: whatever may happen, go on trusting in God; then will be realized—how? 'I know not,' just look at the cross![5]

Jesus is the defenseless one who goes on trusting. In taking seriously the psalmist's maledictory demand that God execute justice, Jesus shows his determination to live in poverty of spirit so that, as Meister Eckhart said, he is so empty of self that God must be the place in which the divine acts. For so long as a person reserves even a place for God to act, let alone a place from which one may act oneself, there is no room for God to enter and act.[6] In the maledictions, the psalms communicate a spirit of absolute trust and obedience that Jesus then manifests with his own life and death. This spirit is identical to that of a song written by John H. Sammis in another era, the second and third verses and chorus of "When We Walk with the Lord."

> Not a burden we bear,
> Not a sorrow we share,
> But our toil he doth richly repay;
> Not a grief or a loss,
> Not a frown or a cross,
> But is blest if we trust and obey.

> But we never can prove
> The delights of his love
> Until all on the altar we lay;
> For the favor he shows
> And the joy he bestows
> Are for them who will trust and obey.

> Trust and obey, for there's no other way
> To be happy in Jesus, but to trust and obey.

Just as Jesus did, the Christian takes the risk of entrusting himself or herself and his or her ultimate validation and vindication to God.

The psalms of lament usually conclude with a vow of praise. Should God vindicate the psalmist, he or she will offer praises to God before the great congregation.

> O my strength, come quickly to my help....

> Then I shall proclaim your name to my brothers,
> praise you in full assembly:
> you who fear Yahweh, praise him!
> Entire race of Jacob, glorify him!
> Entire race of Israel, revere him!
> —Psalm 22:19b, 22–23

Jesus' resurrection and glorification are his fulfillment of this vow of praise. This vindication lies beyond history and cannot be confirmed empirically. Yet the risen Jesus comes to praise God in his concrete existence. John's

Gospel states that Jesus came to "honor" God among humankind. The Greek verb "to honor" can also be translated "to praise." Hence, Jesus the Christ appears in history to praise God in his entire life and death. In his high priestly prayer on the night he was betrayed, Jesus asks, "Father . . . glorify your Son so that your Son may glorify you" (John 17:1). This yearning to praise and to glorify is precisely the yearning of the psalmist. In the lonely places of desolation the psalmist cries out into the darkness, "I waited patiently for the Lord. . . . He drew me up from the desolate pit. . . . He put a new song in my mouth, a song of praise to our God" (Psalm 40:1–3, RSV). Just as the psalmist's intent is to declare God's works and goodness before the congregation of the faithful, John states that Jesus' intent is to "make known the glory of God" in the yet greater congregation of the world. At the end of his high priestly prayer Jesus concludes, "I have made your name known to them and will continue to make it known, so that the love with which you loved me may be in them, and so that I may be in them" (John 17:26). These words are a reflex of the psalmist's vow of praise. Jesus' unflawed fulfillment of the psalmist's promise signals his perception that his deepest destiny was linked to the language of the psalms. Unlike those who went before him and those who followed after, he allowed the psalmist's language to shape so totally his being that his whole life conformed entirely to it.

Like Jesus, we are called to consummate these same vows of praise and obedience. We are to praise God and to declare God's mighty deeds before the world by our own existence.

> Now you too, in him, have heard the message of the truth and the good news of your salvation, and have believed it; and you too have been stamped with the seal of the Holy Spirit of the Promise, the pledge of our inheritance which brings freedom for those whom God has taken for his own, to make his glory praised.
> —Ephesians 1:13–14

Through uniting our praises to the psalmist's praise, we weave our inner selves into the fabric of Christ's own inner life of faith. The more this inner life corresponds to the inner life of Christ, the more our outer lives exhibit the same conformity to Christ's own outer life. This correspondence is decisive for the whole New Testament concept of praise.

> The congregation of Jesus Christ is called on to praise God by standing in the world as followers of Jesus Christ, who praised the Father in his life and death. It praises God by confessing in its whole existence "what God has done for us." In such praise of the congregation, in which and by which it confesses before the world God's deed in Jesus Christ, exactly the same thing happens . . . [as in] the basic, central praise of God in the Psalms: declarative praise. The proclamation of the church can then be only a way in which this praise is expressed by the congregation through its existence. It must fail if it sets out to be something else than the *hōdāh* of the one saved in the declarative Psalms of praise.[7]

Jesus understood who he was and what he was called to become by praying the psalms. He prayed them not as God's word spoken to him from outside, but as a divine word speaking through him from within. The psalms provided the map by means of which he guided himself through not only the wilderness of the temptations, but also the final days of conflict and of confrontation. Even in the hour of his death, Jesus turned to the psalms in order to understand once more what dimension of trusting obedience was demanded of him.

The psalms, infused with this presence of Christ, make accessible and actual for us the full range of Jesus' experience. In praying the psalms, we enter into that world of meaning and find our own wilderness sojourn illuminated and clarified. In praying the psalms we pass through our own hearts to the heart of God as revealed in Jesus' inner life.

Questions for Reflection/Discussion

1. The psalms touch the deepest parts of human experience. Think about the range of emotions represented in the following list. Call to mind a personal experience to represent each one. When you have your experiences clearly in mind, skim the Psalter to find verses that express each emotion in the list. (You may want to jot the reference next to the emotion.) Then, read the verse from the psalms in light of your experience of that emotion.

Fear	Resentment
Despair	Revenge
Courage	Praise
Love	Anger
Hope	Gratitude

In what way does the psalm reflect your own deepest feelings? In what way does it differ? What does the psalm suggest about God in this situation? What does the psalm suggest about the psalmist? As your personal prayer, what does the psalm suggest about you?

2. Choose a psalm that has special meaning for you and read it as your personal prayer. If you allowed your life to be shaped by this psalm, what changes would you have to make? Which ones would be the most difficult? Why? Which ones would be the easiest? Why?

3. If you are studying with a group, share those reflections you are comfortable sharing with one another. If this is a personal study time, you may find it helpful to record your reflections in a journal.

CHAPTER THREE: *Seeing*
New Patterns
in Old Designs

AS THE FIRST Christians prayed the psalms, they experienced them as a many-sided epiphany. The psalms gave those early Christian communities access to the divine nature as it had been revealed to them in the psalmic prayer of Jesus. By praying the prayers that disclosed Jesus' own inner heart and spirit, they opened their own inner lives to the same transforming power. In making themselves receptive to the psalms with the same openness that had characterized Jesus' approach to the psalms, the early church created the opportunity for that divine word embedded within the psalms to transform them as it had transformed Jesus. The psalms gave coherence and wholeness to their dreams and intuitions. The psalms penetrated the pattern of human emotion and aspiration with their own living design. The early Christians, by opening their minds to the yeasty ferment of the psalms, could have in them that mind which was in Christ Jesus. They may have prayed the psalms hundreds of times in crisis and thanksgiving. They may have stood dreamily in the synagogue as the cantor intoned them, barely listening as the cracked and dry words skittered along the stark walls and floor. They may have peered through the wreathed incense and the smoke of boiling flesh or burning lambs as the psalms reverberated in the chambers of the Temple but not within the chambers of their own heart. Suddenly, however, those words were bathed in a new mode of perception. They no longer were just spiritual songs and prayers that spoke of the inherence of guilt and innocence, hope and lament in the hearts of the pious. They no longer hinted at events long ago in the life of David. The psalms certainly did remain all these; but they were suddenly more than these.

39

As an artist paints in oils upon a canvas, he or she occasionally corrects an error by painting over it with another design. The canvas is too expensive to toss aside because a mistake has been made upon it. Sometimes a whole painted canvas will be reused and an entirely different pattern or scene is buried beneath the surface of a now altered painting. Chemical reactions over time will sometimes cause the paint to crack or become transparent and thus reveal an underlying scene.

> Old paint on canvas, as it ages, sometimes becomes transparent. When that happens it is possible, in some pictures, to see the original lines: A tree will show through a woman's dress, a child makes way for a dog, a large boat is no longer on an open sea. That is called pentimento because the painter "repented," changed his mind. Perhaps it would be as well to say that the old conception, replaced by a later choice, is a way of seeing and then seeing again.[1]

The psalms were shot through with *pentimento* for those early Christian communities. Upon the expensive and precious canvas of the divine pathos, the inner movements of God's own passion, the psalms record layer after layer of meaning. As generations of the devout prayed the psalms, new dimensions of meaning cracked open and bestowed a fresh vision. At times the reader experiences the surface design, that emotion first etched upon the psalmist's heart in the beginning. Other times the reader draws a connection to the life of David or to some event in Israel's long history of salvation. Occasionally, through those cracked and timeworn words, badly discolored by generations of use and abuse, a more elemental pattern of meaning is unveiled, a yet decipherable design of experience. This design then casts new light upon the human venture and brings order and harmony to the chaos of our inner lives. The whole sweep of salvation history, of God's yearning for humankind, is discerned beneath the pentimento surface and shimmers upon the very surface of one's own heart. For the early Christians this luminous event occurred when they prayed the psalms as the prayers of Jesus. All the divine pathos was gathered together in the heart of Jesus. All God's yearning and pain in relationship to humanity found an outlet in the psalms. As the church prayed the psalms with fresh eyes and ears, they could taste this divine passion and pattern.

The early church could not resist turning to the psalms at every moment of testimony and of proclamation. At times their use of the Psalter verges on what the modern mind would label abuse. Their methods of interpreting the psalms would be regarded by us as inappropriate. Yet the early communities of Christ found in these pentimento patterns a grammar of existence that enabled them to locate themselves in time and in space. We who are so unsure of our place in the order of reality, who are alienated in many ways not only from the world but from ourselves, might do well to confess our sin of pride and learn from these ancient interpreters.

At Pentecost, Peter turns immediately to the psalms in order to interpret this strange and inexplicable happening. He first explains the event in terms of the promise of Joel 3:1–5 (2:28–32). In the end-time, God will pour out the Spirit upon all flesh. Then Peter immediately turns to the psalms in order to provide a deeper elucidation. In rapid succession he recites portions of Psalms 16, 110, and 132:

> As David says of [the Christ]:

> I saw the Lord before me always,
> for with him at my right hand nothing can shake me.
> So my heart was glad
> and my tongue cried out with joy;
> my body, too, will rest in the hope
> that you will not abandon my soul to Hades
> nor allow your holy one to experience corruption.
> You have made known the way of life to me,
> you will fill me with gladness through your presence.

> Brothers, no one can deny that the patriarch David himself is dead and buried: his tomb is still with us. But since he was a prophet, and knew that God had sworn him an oath to make one of his descendants succeed him on the throne, what he foresaw and spoke about was the resurrection of the Christ: he is the one who was not

abandoned to Hades, and whose body did not experience corruption. God raised this man Jesus to life, and all of us are witnesses to that. Now raised to the heights by God's right hand, he has received from the Father the Holy Spirit, who was promised, and what you see and hear is the outpouring of that Spirit. For David himself never went up to heaven; and yet these words are his:

> The Lord said to my Lord:
> Sit at my right hand
> until I make your enemies
> a footstool for you.

For this reason the whole House of Israel can be certain that God has made this Jesus whom you crucified both Lord and Christ.

—Acts 2:25–36

Arguing from Psalm 16:8–11, Peter asserts that these words cannot possibly apply to David whose "tomb is with us to this day." They can only apply to Jesus whom "God raised up" and to whose resurrection Peter and his associates are witnesses. Peter then utilized Psalm 110:1 to buttress his thesis that David cannot be speaking of himself in these psalms. Jesus, the Risen Lord, must be the "lord" to whom David's Lord and God speaks a promise of victory. This victory, says Peter, is the resurrection. Finally Peter links God's promise of an eternal throne in Psalm 132:11 to Jesus' enthronement. Again, David is dead; so the eternal throne cannot be his. Christ, on the other hand, is risen to eternal life.

Peter at the very birth of the church asserts that the psalms that earlier had been historicized and applied to David are to be applied now to God's new anointed one, Jesus the Crucified. The emotions of the psalms no longer reveal only the inner workings of the human spirit, but they also disclose the spirit and inner life of Jesus.

Whole categories of psalms that were once interpreted only in the light of human experience or of Israel's history are now transformed into disclosures of the divine nature as made known in Jesus, the Word of God. This is particularly true of the laments, the largest category of the psalms. Jesus himself had already pointed the early church in this direction through his application of the laments to himself. Paul's inaugural sermon at Antioch of Pisidia also finds in the psalms rich material for his proclamation of the gospel:

> We have come here to tell you the Good News. It was to our ancestors that God made the promise but it is to us, their children, that he has fulfilled it, by raising Jesus from the dead. As scripture says in the first psalm: "You are my son: today I have become your father." The fact that God raised him from the dead, never to return to corruption, is no more than what he had declared: "To you I shall give the sure and holy things promised to David." This is explained by another text: "You will not allow your holy one to experience corruption." Now when David in his own time had served God's purposes he died; he was buried with his ancestors and has certainly experienced corruption. The one whom God has raised up, however, has not experienced corruption.
>
> —Acts 13:32–37

Paul's sermon revolves around the interpretation of several psalms. In particular Paul discusses Psalm 16 in the terms similar to those that Peter had used. This may be more the result of the editor or editors of Acts than anything else. The sermons, prayers, and speeches of Acts are interwoven and supplement one another. They supply steps in the author's overall argument, expanding and completing one another's thoughts. What is surprising is that Paul is portrayed as finding messianic significance in this same obscure psalm of lament. It indicates the importance that the laments had for the early church, as well as the processes at work in drawing the psalms as a whole into the church's orbit.

These laments often strike the modern ear as offensive in their extravagant protests of innocence and their self-serving promises to God. They raise, however, a much more profound question. They pose what we in our modern way of thinking call the question of life's meaning. It is the cry that rises forth from anguish and disappointment: "Why?" We might say it through the mediation of different words and concepts, but the experience is identical. All whose lives have been shattered by crises know the psalmist's pleading complaint as their own. The same cry takes shape on our own lips: "How long, O Lord?" "Why me?" In these protests against suffering the early church perceived beneath their cracked, transparent, pentimento surface another web of significance.

The psalms of lament are songs of painful relinquishment in times when one's personal world is collapsing. They do not emerge out of situations of calm repose. "Rather, people are driven to such poignant prayer and song as are found in the Psalter precisely by *experiences of dislocation and relocation*."[2] The laments speak of being cast into the pit. This is not so different from when we say that we are in the pits: times of powerlessness, abandonment, helplessness, times when our dearest hopes and dreams have been defeated.

> Turn to me and show me thy favour,
> for I am lonely and oppressed.
>   Relieve the sorrows of my heart
>   and bring me out of my distress
>   —Psalm 25:16–17, NEB

Hear me and answer,
    for my cares give me no peace.
I am panic-stricken at the shouts of my enemies,
    at the shrill clamour of the wicked;
for they heap trouble on me
    and they revile me in their anger.
My heart is torn with anguish
    and the terrors of death come upon me.
Fear and trembling overwhelm me
    and I shudder from head to foot.
Oh that I had the wings of a dove
    to fly away and be at rest!
            —Psalm 55:2–6, NEB

I lay sweating and nothing would cool me;
I refused all comfort.
When I called God to mind, I groaned;
as I lay thinking, darkness came over my spirit.
My eyelids were tightly closed;
I was dazed and I could not speak.
My thoughts went back to times long past,

I remembered forgotten years;
all night long I was in deep distress,
as I lay thinking, my spirit was sunk in despair.
—Psalm 77:2b–6, NEB

Despite their bitter distress, the laments do not end in despair or cynicism. They continue to hope against hope. They assert that even as one descends into the pits one may rise up as on the wings of a dove. They affirm that God hears supplicants even in the pit and lifts them up. Jonah, fleeing from God, is cast into the stormy waters and descends down to the very base of the cosmic mountain. Even there God hears his cry and draws him back up to life. This motif of descent and ascent regularly appears in the psalms.

When the bonds of death held me fast,
destructive torrents overtook me,
the bonds of Sheol tightened round me,
the snares of death were set to catch me. . . .

[God] reached down from the height and took me,
[God] drew me out of mighty waters.
—Psalm 18:4–5, 16, NEB

Save me, O God;
for the waters have risen up to my neck.
I sink in muddy depths and have no foothold;
I am swept into deep water,
and the flood carries me away. . . .

But by thy saving power, O God, lift me high
above my pain and my distress,
then I will praise God's name in song
and glorify [God] with thanksgiving.
—Psalm 69:1–2, 29–30, NEB

O LORD, the ocean lifts up, the ocean lifts up its
clamour;
the ocean lifts up its pounding waves.
The LORD on high is mightier far
than the noise of great waters,
mightier than the breakers of the sea.
—Psalm 93:3–4, NEB

The psalms attest that the God who rules even the pits of life hears those who cry for help.

> Rather, the power of God brings us out of the pit to new life which is not the same as pre-pit existence. When one is in the pit, one cannot believe or imagine that good can come again. For that reason, the psalmist finally focuses not on the pit but on the One who rules there and everywhere.[3]

The laments focus not so much on the specific illness or condition of the supplicant but rather plead that the order and meaning of reality as proclaimed in the tradition be extended and manifested in one particular situation.

As the early church read these psalms, they saw in them the experience of Jesus as a model of this same descent and ascent. The motif of descent and ascent is drawn into the orbit of the much more powerful motif of death and resurrection. Like Jonah or the psalmists, Jesus of Nazareth descends into the swirling waters of chaos, disorder, and death. Yet the one who has demonstrated utter loyalty to God's will and has shown himself to be a perfect servant of that divine will is not allowed to suffer corruption. God raises him up and gives him victory as the Christ of God. This victory belongs only to God because only God as creator has dominion over chaos.

Death and chaos are always portrayed in the psalms as watery powers. This is a general assumption throughout the poetic language and mythology of the ancient Near East. In the beginning all is a primordial, chaotic sea, *tehom*, according to the priestly author of Genesis. In the Babylonian creation epic, Marduk triumphs over the primordial dragon, *Tiamat*. Both *tehom* and *Tiamat* stem from the same root and probably represent the same generalized concept. Several passages in the Hebrew Bible allude to this elemental contest between Yahweh, the God of Israel, and the dragon of chaos. God fights a terrible battle against Rahab, or Leviathan, or simply, "the dragon."

> Yet, God, my king from the first,
> author of saving acts throughout the earth,

by your power you split the sea in two,
and smashed the heads of monsters on the waters.

You crushed Leviathan's heads,
leaving him for wild animals to eat,
you opened the spring, the torrent,
you dried up inexhaustible rivers.

—Psalm 74:12–15

By his power he stilled the sea;
　by his understanding he smote Rahab.
By his wind the heavens were made fair;
　his hand pierced the fleeing serpent.

—Job 26:12–13, RSV

In Isaiah 27:1 (RSV), Leviathan is called "the fleeing serpent
...the twisting serpent...the dragon that is in the sea." In
these mythic battles the defeat of the dragon leads into
the god's creation of the world. The deity then takes
steps to insure that chaos will never again break loose
upon the world. Humanity can live in safety and give
thanks. The psalms utilize this universal language of
creation.

Bless Yahweh, my soul. . . .

At your reproof the waters took to flight,
they fled at the sound of your thunder,
cascading over the mountains, into the valleys,
down to the reservoir you made for them;
you imposed the limits they must never cross again,
or they would once more flood the land.

—Psalm 104:1a, 7–9

Israel's description of its Exodus from Egypt employs this
same complex of images and metaphors. God commands
the waters of chaos to part while the people of Israel pass
out of the pit of slavery in Egypt. Then God allows the
waters to revert to their natural disorder, and they overwhelm the Egyptians in death and destruction.

Jesus also must descend into the watery deeps of death
and disorder. All Israel's prior experience of destruction
and death, symbolized in the psalmist's metaphor of
water, is recapitulated in Jesus' descent into the grave.

The church, the New Israel, perceived that in Jesus' victory over death God had achieved a breakthrough as significant as the one at the world's genesis or at Israel's Exodus from Egypt. The psalmist's longing for a world in which one could dwell in absolute safety found its satisfaction in Jesus the Christ. Whereas Israel had continued to be subject to periodic eruptions of disorder because of its failure to trust absolutely God's faithfulness, Jesus remained true to the vision of pure obedience. In so doing he overcame all Israel's failure in obedience and won a new and final victory over the dragons of chaos.

> After that will come the end, when he hands over the kingdom to God the Father, having done away with every sovereignty, authority and power. For he must be king until he has put all his enemies under his feet and the last of the enemies to be destroyed is death, for everything is to be put under his feet.—Though when it is said that everything is subjected, this clearly cannot include the One who subjected everything to him. And when everything is subjected to him, then the Son himself will be subject in his turn to the One who subjected all things to him, so that God may be all in all.
> —1 Corinthians 15:24–28

The ancient psalms of lament now come together around the model of Jesus' descent and ascent. In praying them as the prayers of Jesus, the Christian community participates in a whole history of dislocation and relocation that finally culminates in Jesus' definitive triumph over death and disorder.

The early church drew this constellation of meaning into its baptismal symbolism. Water becomes the symbol for the chaotic forces of diminishment and dissolution into which the believer must descend. The Christian descends into the watery pit; but, as with Christ, the Christian is lifted up and given a new nature by a gracious God:

> Do you not know that all of us who have been baptized into Christ Jesus were baptized into his death? We were buried therefore with him by baptism into death, so that as

Christ was raised from the dead by the glory of the Father,
we too might walk in newness of life.
For if we have been united with him in a death like his,
we shall certainly be united with him in a resurrection like
his. We know that our old self was crucified with him so
that the sinful body might be destroyed, and we might no
longer be enslaved to sin. For he who has died is freed
from sin. But if we have died with Christ, we believe that
we shall also live with him.

—Romans 6:3–8, RSV

In our baptism, we participate not only in the dying
and rising of Christ, but we are drawn into the healing of
a more fundamental cosmic disorder. God's call to Abraham follows sometime after the scattering of the peoples
at the tower of Babel. Israel's election and history were
meant as a means of blessing to overcome the curse that
had fallen upon humanity. This curse begins in the garden with Adam and Eve, says the writer of Genesis.
Following that event come a series of human failures that
widen progressively humanity's alienation from itself and
from God: the murder of Abel, the corruption prior to the
flood, the building of the tower. Israel is meant to heal
this broken and alienated condition. Because of its inability to trust, however, Israel itself becomes subject to the
tragic eruptions of dissolution and decay. The psalms
allude to this frustrating of the divine economy of salvation and yearn for the perfect obedience necessary to heal
and to mend the ruptured cosmos.
When they prayed the psalms as the prayers of Jesus,
the early church experienced itself as participating directly in Jesus' own movement from security to the place of
poverty and powerlessness. They were also one with him
in his ascent from the pit to the place of utter safety. In
praying the psalms, the church prayed and lived in union
with Christ as his collapse of hope and purpose turned
into fruition and realization. They could share in his
cosmic healing and experience a dimension of that healing within themselves as they entered into the psalms as
the inner prayer life of Jesus. In ways not even perceived
by Jesus the various elements of the psalms had become
attached to his personal history, enriching and extending

the meaning of life for those who identified with him. The psalms of lament acquired their full meaning in the light of Jesus' descent and ascent, a rhythm repeated once by every Christian in baptism and made real in every recitation of the psalms.

The One who rules the pit is also the One enthroned on high. The early church could draw a direct connection between the psalms of praise and lament and those of Yahweh's enthronement. The enthronement psalms form a distinct body within the Psalter. All share in the common acclaim, "Yahweh is king." This kingship stems from God's subduing the powers of chaos. The One who conquered the dragons of chaos at the beginning of time is indeed the One to whom the believer cries when drawn down into the watery mire. The believer pleas for that ordering power manifested at creation to be concretized in this particular situation. The old cultic cries "The Lord is king" no longer apply just to Yahweh, but also to Jesus, who has recapitulated Yahweh's victory over dissolution and disorder by his victory over death. The songs of enthronement become songs of Easter joy for the Christian church.

> Sing Yahweh a new song
>   for he has performed marvels,
> his own right hand, his holy arm,
>   gives him the power to save.
>
> Yahweh has displayed his power;
>   has revealed his righteousness to the nations,
> mindful of his love and faithfulness
>   to the house of Israel. . . .
>
> to the sound of trumpet and horn
>   acclaim Yahweh the King!
>
> Let the sea thunder and all that it holds,
>   and the world, with all who live in it;
> let all the rivers clap their hands
>   and the mountains shout for joy,
>
> at the presence of Yahweh, for he comes
>   to judge the earth,

> to judge the world with righteousness
> and the nations with strict justice.
> —Psalm 98:1–3, 6–9

The chaotic waters of death, sea and river, must submit to God's power and praise God. Jesus' victory has completed the cosmos's subjugation to the power of God. Therefore, Christians can be certain that

> neither death, nor life, nor angels, nor principalities, nor things present, nor things to come, nor powers, nor height, nor depth, nor anything else in all creation, will be able to separate us from the love of God in Christ Jesus our Lord.
> —Romans 8:38–39 RSV

Paul's hymn grows out of his experiencing the psalms through the inner life of Jesus. Even in death Jesus could trust in the One who is enthroned over the flood.

> Out of my distress I called on the Lord;
> the Lord answered me and set me free.
> With the Lord on my side I do not fear.
> What can man do to me?
> —Psalm 118:5–6, RSV

In praying the psalms as the prayers of Jesus we also can learn to trust when there seem no grounds for trust. Victory belongs to the God who has subjected all things, even death, to his power. Martin Luther's first major work was a study of the psalms. In praying the psalms Luther allowed the word nestled within them to form his person as Christ had allowed himself to be shaped by the spirit of the psalms. In praying the psalms Luther conformed his voice and being to the voice and being of the psalms. His hymn "A Mighty Fortress Is Our God" gives evidence that he could face life with that confidence, courage, and trust that characterized Jesus and the psalmists.

> A mighty fortress is our God,
> A bulwark never failing;

> Our helper he amid the flood
> Of mortal ills prevailing:
> For still our ancient foe
> Doth seek to work us woe;
> His craft and power are great,
> And, armed with cruel hate,
> On earth is not his equal.

> And though this world, with devils filled,
> Should threaten to undo us,
> We will not fear, for God hath willed
> His truth to triumph through us:
> The Prince of Darkness grim,
> We tremble not for him;
> His rage we can endure,
> for lo, his doom is sure;
> One little word shall fell him.

These same enthronement psalms drew to themselves another node of meaning in the early church. At the Areopagus, Paul preached upon the enthronement psalms. Paul begins by quoting to the Athenians verses from their own poets, "In him we live and move and have our being" (Acts 17:28, RSV). This means, explains Paul, that God's person and rule are universal. The God of whom the poet speaks is a God who rules the whole universe and cannot be limited by representations of gold or silver, stone or even concepts. Then Paul refers to two of the enthronement psalms, Psalms 95:13 and 98:9.

> Then shall all the trees of the wood sing for joy
>   before the Lord, for he comes,
>   for he comes to judge the earth.
> He will judge the world with righteousness,
>   and the peoples with his truth.
>   —Psalm 96:12b–13, RSV

> Let the floods clap their hands;
>   let the hills sing for joy together
> before the Lord, for he comes
>   to judge the earth.
> He will judge the world with righteousness,
>   and the peoples with equity.
>   —Psalm 98:8–9, RSV

Paul concludes that the time of this judgment are at hand,

because he has fixed a day on which he will judge the
world in righteousness by a man whom he has appointed,
and of this he has given assurance to all men by raising
him from the dead.

—Acts 17:31, RSV

The enthronement psalms thus become part of the
early church's authorization for its Gentile mission and
an integral element in its sense of universal mission. If
Yahweh is a universal God who has subjected all things
through Christ, then the history of salvation no longer
focuses upon Israel alone, but rather must encompass all
nations and peoples. Those who previously were separated
"have now been brought near in the blood of Christ. For
he is our peace, who has made us both one, and has
broken down the dividing wall of hostility" (Eph. 2:13b–14,
RSV). The glory of enthronement, however, cannot be
separated from Jesus' passion and death.

Thus the enthronement psalms naturally fuse themselves with the psalms of lament within the early church's
experience. The church could wed both categories into a
total design of death, resurrection/ascension, and final
glorification. The Son of Man who suffers and dies will
be the same Son of Man who is given dominion and glory
and kingdom by the Ancient of Days and who will come
again on clouds of glory to judge all things (Dan. 7:11–14,
26–27).

If the laments could express Jesus' inner emotions
during the passion, then the psalms of enthronement
could give voice to his experience of resurrection/ascension
and to his final enthronement in glory. While the hymn
fragments of the New Testament are largely a product of
hellenistic Jewish Christianity, they are grounded in the
forms and symbols of these psalms.

His state was divine, yet he did not cling to his equality
with God but emptied himself to assume the condition of a
slave, and became as men are; and being as all men are,
he was humbler yet, even to accepting death, death on a
cross. But God raised him high and gave him the name
which is above all other names so that all beings in the
heavens, on earth and in the underworld, should bend
the knee at the name of Jesus and that every tongue

should acclaim Jesus Christ as Lord, to the glory of God the Father.

—Philippians 2:6–11

He is the radiant light of God's glory and the perfect copy of his nature, sustaining the universe by his powerful command; and now that he has destroyed the defilement of sin, he has gone to take his place in heaven at the right hand of divine Majesty.

—Hebrews 1:3

Christ himself, innocent though he was, had died once for sins, died for the guilty, to lead us to God. In the body he was put to death, in the spirit he was raised to life, and, in the spirit, he went to preach to the spirits in prison. . . . [Jesus Christ] has entered heaven and is at God's right hand, now that he has made the angels and Dominations and Powers his subjects.

—1 Peter 3:18–19, 22

These same motifs continued to exercise their influence upon the early church as it forged its faith in response to the heretical currents and bitter conflicts of the fourth century. Anchored in its experience of the psalms as the prayers of Jesus the Christ, the church affirmed repeatedly that only the One who suffered under Pontius Pilate, was crucified, and buried could be the One who ascended into heaven, is seated at God's right hand, and will come from there to judge the living and the dead.

It is the same complex of shared memory and experience that the contemporary church celebrates on the last Sunday after Pentecost, at the Feast of Christ the King, when it prays:

> All-powerful God,
> your only Son came to earth
>   in the form of a slave
>   and is now enthroned at your right hand,
>   where he rules in glory.
> As he reigns as King in our hearts,
>   may we rejoice in his peace,
>   glory in his justice,
>   and live in his love.
> For with you and the Holy Spirit
>   he rules now and for ever. Amen.[4]

Questions for Reflection/Discussion

1. Take a few moments to think about *trust*. Why do we trust some persons and not others? What qualities encourage us to trust another person?

2. Examine the Psalter to locate verses that may speak of these same qualities. What, then, does it mean to trust God as the psalmist did? As Jesus did?

3. Think of an experience you have had of "dying and rising," of "descending and ascending." How is your experience similar to those expressed in the psalms? In what way might it differ? How do the expressions of God's faithfulness in the psalms relate to your experience of "dying and rising"? In what ways might these expressions be helpful to you in the future?

4. After spending some time reflecting upon the questions, record your insights in your journal or share them with a partner from your study group.

CHAPTER FOUR: *Cracking Open the Hardened Shell*

ALTHOUGH THE PSALTER was not officially recognized as a part of the authoritative Jewish canon of scripture until about A.D. 90 when the Pharisees met at Jamnia following the destruction of Jerusalem, the psalms have left their imprint everywhere in the first-century world. The psalms of Solomon are thought to be a product of certain Pharisees who sought to carry on the tradition of psalm composition. The Qumran community's scroll of thanksgiving hymns bears witness to that community's attempt to live a life steeped in the psalms as well as to create new psalms. The hymns and canticles incorporated into the early chapters of Luke's Gospel, as well as those hymns to Christ that are scattered through Paul's letters, manifest this same love of the psalms and respect for the Psalter's inspiration.

In this environment, there was no hesitancy about ascribing Davidic authorship to the psalms. Frequently the single word "David" was a synonym for the Psalter. Through the mouth of David, God had spoken the divine word. It was only natural, then, for the early church to draw the specifically Davidic or royal psalms into its understanding of Jesus.

Peter's Pentecost sermon turns upon two royal psalms (Acts 2:14–36). Psalm 132 is a magnificent hymn glorifying the Davidic king. It celebrates God's eternal promises to David and to Zion.

> A prince of your own line
>   will I set upon your throne.
> If your sons keep my covenant
>   and heed the teaching that I give them,
> their sons in turn for all time

shall sit upon your throne.
For the Lord has chosen Zion. . . .

There I will renew the line of David's house
and light a lamp for my anointed king;
his enemies will I clothe with shame,
but on his head shall be a shining crown.
—Psalm 132:11b–13, 17–18, NEB

Peter preaches that the old Davidic line had come to an
end because it had sinned against God and had neither
trusted God nor kept the covenant law. A promise,
however, is a promise. Somehow God must honor God's
vow. In Jesus, born of David's house, the old promise of
an eternal throne is renewed and completed. Proof of this
election is the resurrection. A shining crown has been set
upon Jesus' head while his enemies have been put to
shame. As the Davidic king in Psalm 18 could cry out and
plead for God to lift him from the deep waters of death,
so now this cry for salvation finds an answer in Jesus'
being raised up from the dead.

Jesus himself had already prepared the path for this
clustering of the royal psalms around him. He had applied to himself the royal adoption formula of Psalm 2.
The early Christian communities simply drew out the
implications of this identification. Many royal psalms
contained themes amenable to Jesus' passion. The king is
threatened with defeat or humiliation. An unexpected
victory that can only be ascribed to God's miraculous
intervention then saves the king at the very last moment.

Now I know that Yahweh
saves his anointed,
and answers him from his holy heaven
with mighty victories from his own right hand.

Some boast of chariots, some of horses,
but we boast about the name of Yahweh our God.
—Psalm 20:6–7

Yahweh, the king rejoices in your power. . . .

For you have met him with choicest blessings,
put a crown of pure gold on his head;

he asked for life, and you give it him,
length of days for ever and ever.

Great is his glory through your saving help,
you have loaded him with splendor and majesty;
yes, you confer on him everlasting blessings,
you gladden him with the joy of your presence.
—Psalm 21:1, 3–6

Psalms 2, 45, 72, 89, 101, and 144 also develop this theme
under a variety of metaphors. Jesus becomes the new
anointed one, adopted as God's own son. He is brought
to the verge of humiliation and defeat. Death encompasses
him. At the last moment Yahweh intervenes and vindi-
cates the loyal son and servant. All the royal associations
of the Psalter thus find a place within the early church's
understanding of Jesus' life and ministry.

Peter's reference to Psalm 110 is a further illustration of
this royal tradition's reinterpretation. The text of Psalm
110 has suffered greatly in transmission. Even in ancient
times it was difficult to read, let alone understand. This
very obscurity encouraged speculation. Its reference to
Melchizedek, one of the Bible's more mysterious and
obscure figures, heightened this text's appeal. Melchizedek
appears in Genesis 14 as king of Salem and as priest of
God Most High. After Abraham has defeated the kings of
the East, Melchizedek comes forth with bread and wine
to bless Abraham. Following this blessing, Abraham gives
to Melchizedek one-tenth of all the booty he has captured.
Melchizedek then disappears from the pages of the Hebrew Bible as mysteriously and as abruptly as he had first
appeared. Salem itself remains an unknown city. Later
writers sometimes identified it with Jerusalem. In the
narrative Melchizedek is clearly Abraham's superior. Eventually the theologians of the Davidic monarchy brought
Melchizedek into their formulations of a royal theology.
He becomes the prototype for the Davidic monarchy. Just
as he was both priest and king, so the Davidic monarchs
exercise both these functions. The Davidic king was the
successor to the order of Melchizedek. To say that Jesus is
a priest forever after the order of Melchizedek was to
make a broad and sweeping claim for Jesus' status. The

Book of Hebrews would later make much of this identification of Jesus with the eternal priesthood of Melchizedek. Jesus offered up prayers and anguished pleas "to him who was able to save from death." Because of his "godly fear" Jesus' cries were answered.

> Although he was a Son, he learned obedience through what he suffered; and being made perfect he became the source of eternal salvation to all who obey him, being designated by God a high priest after the order of Melchizedek.
>
> —Hebrews 5:8–11, RSV

The author has drawn together in a brilliant way the royal images of Psalm 110 (a priest forever) with the psalms of laments (loud cries and tears) and the psalms of enthronement (to him who was able to save).

Later in Acts, Peter and John are brought before the high priest Annas, Caiaphas, and the whole council because of their preaching. In their defense, they turn, once again, to the psalms. This defense illuminates yet another line of early Christian approach to the psalms. Their proclamation, Peter and John claim, is based upon Psalm 118:22. "This is the stone which was rejected by you builders, but which has become the head of the corner" (Acts 4:11, RSV).

> No, I shall not die, I shall live
>   to recite the deeds of Yahweh;
> though Yahweh has punished me often,
>   he has not abandoned me to Death.
>
> Open the gates of virtue to me,
>   I will come in and give thanks to Yahweh.
> This is Yahweh's gateway,
>   through which the virtuous may enter.
> I thank you for having heard me,
>   you have been my savior.
>
> It was the stone rejected by the builders
> that proved to be the keystone;
> this is Yahweh's doing
> and it is wonderful to see.

> This is the day made memorable by Yahweh,
> what immense joy for us!
>
> —Psalm 118:17–24

The psalmist's ancient victory song has become an Easter hymn to the Risen One. This identification of Jesus with the rejected one who in the end triumphs allowed the early church to apply those themes of reversal of fortune to Jesus.

This was already a familiar theme in Jesus' own preaching. In Luke's Gospel, Jesus thanks God that truth has been withdrawn from the wise while understanding has been given to small children (Luke 10:21). Lazarus the beggar will rest in Abraham's bosom while the rich man who ignored him will suffer eternal torment. In the kingdom of God, the rich will be sent away empty while the hungry will be filled with good things (Luke 1:53). Those who seek to be first at the banquet table will be last, while those who are last will be first.

This great reversal theme has a long history in Israel. It probably emerged from the laments for the dead. Later generations then applied it as a plea for the living as well as the dead. Eventually it came to include both the personal and the collective dimensions. Not only could the fortunes of an individual be reversed, but so could those of whole populations. The Song of Hannah illustrates one of the finest early uses of this theme.

> The bows of the mighty are broken,
>   but the feeble gird on strength.
> Those who were full have hired themselves out for bread,
>   but those who were hungry have ceased to hunger.
> The barren has borne seven,
>   but she who has many children is forlorn.
> The Lord kills and brings to life;
>   he brings down to Sheol and raises up.
> The Lord makes poor and makes rich;
>   he brings low, he also exalts.
> He raises up the poor from the dust;
>   he lifts the needy from the ash heap
> to make them sit with princes
>   and inherit a seat of honor.
>
> —1 Samuel 2:4–8a, RSV

Peter and John, along with the first Christian communities, see this history of God's reversal in fortunes as summed up and consummated in the history of Jesus. He is the perfect example for this reversal. Those who find their lives in union with him now experience the same gracious action of dislocation and relocation, wounding and healing, dying and rising. In praying the psalms, the Christian can vicariously participate in this same rhythm.

When Peter and John are released from arrest, they express their thanks in reciting the psalms. They sing Psalm 146:6. This psalm of praise amplifies upon the theme of the great reversal. Those who are imprisoned will be free. Those who are blind will see. The hungry are filled with good things. The oppressors of the poor will stand in the place of judgment (Acts 4:23–31). The early church learned from the psalms its grammar of praise. In praying the psalms as the prayers of Jesus, it recovered a language of genuine praise. Their praise arose out of their experience of continued trust in the face of certain defeat. Confident that the God who subdued the dragons of chaos and death was in absolute control of the cosmos, they could praise God in every circumstance.

> Happy is he whose help is the God of Jacob,
>   whose hope is in the Lord his God,
> who made heaven and earth,
>   the sea and all that is in them;
>
> who keeps faith for ever;
>   who executes justice for the oppressed;
>   who gives food to the hungry.
>   —Psalm 146:5–7, RSV

We should not dismiss too lightly this mode of being in the world. We, who often are so dull and sluggish in our outlook, might recover a sense of wonder and a capacity for pleasure were we to drink deeply this inner confidence and vital energy of the psalms. Those who realize the governing image of life is one of tender care that nothing is lost are those free to live life zestfully. Gathered into God's own life, our lives take on another dimension. God passes judgment upon the world. It is, however, "the judgment of a tenderness which loses nothing that can be saved. It is also the judgment of a wisdom which uses what in the temporal world is mere wreckage."[1]

Stephen's sermon, which eventually precipitates his martyrdom, also grounds itself in the psalms. Stephen begins with a long recitation of salvation history. This condensation of the Torah is modeled along the lines found in Psalms 78, 105, or 106. Like Peter, Stephen turns finally to Psalm 132. Whereas Peter had stressed the eternal election of a Davidic king, Stephen stressed the election of Zion and the Temple. This Temple upon Mt. Zion undergoes a radical shift in meaning. Stephen understands the references to Zion no longer in terms of a sacred space, but rather as a sacred person. He takes the references to Zion and the Temple as allusions to one mode of God's being. They refer to God as tabernacling among the people of God. The old imperfect tenting of God's real presence in Zion has been replaced by a new and perfect presence: Christ's own body is the new Temple. All the allusions to holy space in Israel's literature are taken as testimonials to Christ. In the Exodus, Israel was led by the pillar and the cloud. Later God communicated with the people through the Ark and the Tent of Meeting. Finally, under David and Solomon, the Temple was built to provide a stable, permanent place for God to dwell. All these forms of presence, Stephen then proclaims, were merely artificial shadows, cast by human craft. In the fullness of time God has provided the consummate form of divine presence: Jesus. Stephen then concludes by affirming that "the Most High does not dwell in houses made with hands" (Acts 7:48a, RSV). Only the person of Jesus is the perfect dwelling place for God.

Stephen and his accusers are both pondering the ancient problem of God's immanence and transcendence. How can God be in this particular place and moment if God is a universal God? How can I know myself protected and cared for when God is unseen? Israel's neighbors had tried to resolve this dilemma by building a temple in which their gods lived. From this house a god could dispense power and blessings. The divine blessings, which were very much concerned with the normal welfare of the people's herds and crops, flowed out from this temple to make fertile the land. Israel came into contact with these religions after it settled in the promised land. It absorbed many of these beliefs into its own faith.

With the establishment of the Davidic monarchy in the old Jebusite city of Jerusalem, the interaction of these two traditions became critical. The Canaanite temple traditions came into sharp conflict with Israel's desert traditions, where God was an unseen but mysterious presence in pillar and cloud, tent and ark. When David announced his intention to build a house for Yahweh, the prophet Nathan acted as representative of the old traditions and protested. Nathan stated that "of old God dwelt directly with the people and needed no house." It was God who provided a house for David and for Israel. They were acting presumptuously and showing a lack of trust in God's faithfulness. If God promised that he would remain present to the chosen people, then God would remain present. Israel did not need to try to box God in or to control how God would be present.

Nonetheless the Temple was built. It became a visible symbol for God's life-giving presence. Israel saw that in its Temple it could control the divine blessings. A fertilizing river flowed from Zion to bring life to the land.

> Praise is rightfully yours,
>   God in Zion. . . .
>
> You visit the earth and water it,
>   you load it with riches;
> God's rivers brim with water
>   to provide their grain.
>
> This is how you provide it:
> by drenching its furrows, by leveling its ridges,
> by softening it with showers, by blessing the first fruits.
> You crown the year with your bounty,
> abundance flows wherever you pass.
>   —Psalm 65:1, 9–11

Psalm 46:4, Isaiah 33:21, Joel 3:8, Ezekiel 47, and Zechariah 14:8 all elaborate upon this river of blessing that flows from Zion and the Temple.

Assyria's destruction of the northern kingdom (Samaria) in 722 B.C. shattered the people's confidence in this simple scheme of things. Refugees from the north knew that the Temple as God's house had not brought unconditional protection. A new school of thought, the Deuteronomic school, arose and asserted that only God's *name* dwelt in the Temple. Through God's *name* God was present to Israel without ever leaving the heavenly realms. This theology enabled Israel and Judah to survive the exile in Babylon without loss of faith. The Temple in Jerusalem fell in 587 B.C. God's name had no resting place; but God still ruled supreme in the cosmos.

Following the exile, the priestly school made a new attempt to resolve the tension between God's presence with the people and God's transcendence. They replaced the Deuteronomic name theology with a theology of the indwelling *glory* of God. Future hope for Israel demanded that the glory return. This glory would bring blessing with it. True existence for Israel was possible only if this glory were dwelling in its midst. For this to occur, the restored community had to be a place fit for the glory of God. Once the people were holy as God is holy, then God could be present in their midst. "Say to all the congregation of the people of Israel, You shall be holy; for I the Lord your God am holy" (Lev. 19:2, RSV). This approach was also flawed by a lack of trust. Israel could not wait in emptiness and poverty for God's goodness to flow into it. It felt driven to take matters into its own hands, to manipulate God and to control the blessings.

Stephen exhorts his hearers that even this priestly approach is now a dead end. It has not solved the problem of remaining open to God's blessings without grasping at them. Stephen then proclaims that the only answer is offered by the One whom those same priests and scribes delivered over to death. Jesus' own body is the new tabernacling and life-giving presence in the people's midst.

The Word has become flesh and tabernacled in the people's midst, full of grace and truth. This tabernacling Word has made known the unknown Creator. Upon Christ's body angels descend and ascend. He is the new link between heaven and earth (John 1:51). Reserving no place within himself for his own self-consciousness, Jesus became that perfect emptiness in which God could act and through which God could be fully manifest. The individual Christian, following Christ's pattern of self-emptying poverty, creates the free and open inner space in which God can come and dwell. The psalms teach that it is God's very nature to wish to be enfleshed. After defeating chaos and decay, God pours life into creation. God spins out worlds and molds matter into living creatures. The true Temple is not a building. It is the human heart made vacant of self. "For we are the temple of the living God; as God said, 'I will live in them and move among them, and I will be their God, and they shall be my people,'" (2 Cor. 6:16, RSV). Christ is the first fruit and the cornerstone "in whom the whole structure is joined together and grows into a holy temple in the Lord; in whom you also are built into it for a dwelling place of God in the Spirit" (Eph. 2:21–22, RSV). Mark's Gospel describes reality when it chronicles how the Temple's veil was torn when Jesus died. Jesus' own body, obedient and selfless even unto death on a cross, has superseded the Temple as a means of divine presence. God's blessings no longer flow from a sacred place but from a sacred person.

The most powerful and poetic expression of this is in the Book of Revelation. In the restored and renewed Holy City there will be no Temple. No Temple is required for the divine blessings to gush forth. God will dwell in the people's midst.

And I saw no temple in the city, for its temple is the Lord God the Almighty and the Lamb. And the city has no need of sun or moon to shine upon it, for the glory of God is its light and its lamp is the Lamb. By its light shall the nations walk; and the kings of the earth shall bring their glory into it, and its gates shall never be shut by day. . . .

Then he showed me the river of the water of life, bright as crystal, flowing from the throne of God and of the Lamb through the middle of the street of the city; also, on either side of the river, the tree of life with its twelve kinds of fruit, yielding its fruit each month; and the leaves of the tree were for the healing of the nations.

—Revelation 21:22–25, 22:1–2, RSV

John the Seer has taken the old Zion hymns and transformed them into a praise and thanksgiving hymn directed to the Lamb, the crucified and risen Jesus.

Jesus himself may have suggested this train of thought to his disciples. "Destroy this temple, and in three days I will raise it up" (John 2:19, RSV). Stephen's speech and the Seer's lyric imagery demonstrate how the early church could take an idea found in germinal form in Jesus' own thought and then elaborate it into a much richer and far more complex pattern of thought. This elaborate web of metaphor and symbol made available a new mode of being-in-the-world to the early church. As they read the songs and psalms of Zion, they saw them crack open. Out of these fissures poured forth previously hidden dimensions of meaning. The psalms of Zion celebrated God's gracious election of Israel and God's decision to bless this people with divine life. The blessing was no longer a partial and limited one, cluttered by brick and stone, human pride and presumption. Grace and healing now was available to all people, offering life abundant to all those who followed the Christ.

Questions for Reflection/Discussion

1. The "great reversal" theme is gaining fresh recognition today in light of the critical issues of peace and justice. Take a few moments to read refletively Psalm 118:17–24, Psalm 146:5–6, and First Samuel 2:4–8. In what ways are you among the oppressed of the world? In what ways might you be an oppressor?

2. Considering your reflections on the previous question, what implications do you see for your own lifestyle? How might the message of the psalms shape your commitments?

3. Discuss your reflections on these questions with your group partner or write about them in your journal. Pay attention to the directions in which your reflection/discussion/journaling move you.

CHAPTER FIVE: *Hearing the Echo of a Forgotten Voice*

BY THE CLOSE of the apostolic era, all the varied themes contained within the Psalter had been drawn into the early church's understanding of Christ's passion and resurrection. In its cruder and more popular forms, this process treated the psalms as mere prophecies of the Messiah. These interpreters considered neither that the psalmists themselves had felt deeply their joy and sorrow, nor that the psalms were expressions of human experience. They were merely prophets who had predicted Christ's birth, life, passion, and resurrection. This argument remained popular through the medieval period and persists in some circles today.

At best, however, the church fathers and mothers saw in the psalms a delicate analogy of being. In his *Philosophical Investigations*, Ludwig Wittgenstein offers a useful hint when he draws attention to the significance of what at first seems quite childish: puzzle pictures. A page is covered with random lines and dots. One person may see a rabbit's head facing left; another, a duck's head facing right. One person may see a lamp stand; another, two human faces looking at one another. Wittgenstein spoke of this phenomenon as "seeing as." You see it as your mind interprets it. One can then expand this notion to that of "experiencing as" not only visually, but through all the organs of perception. We experience situations in different ways, as having different meanings, as requiring different responses. In Israel, the prophets experienced certain historical events as directly shaped by God's sovereign action. Many of their contemporaries experienced the same events without significance. The same is true of the early church and the psalms. In the bitter laments with their pleas for redemption, in the hymns of joyous praise, in the royal psalms through which the king cried out for divine protection, the early church saw a sometimes broken and often transparent pentimento surface. Moreover, this pentimento was not just any painting of trees and birds, ships upon the sea, or stout peasants along country roads. It was a window into another dimension of being.

The psalms were an elaborate picture puzzle. The Jewish community, which had stared into their designs for centuries, could only experience the psalms as they had always done. The early church, its perceptions shattered and reshaped by Jesus' death and resurrection, brought a new vision to the psalms. The emotions expressed so poignantly and so powerfully in the psalms opened the doorway through which they could enter into Christ's own bitter descent and victorious ascent. The luminous ambiguity of these psalms allowed the church to experience them as the very prayers of their own Lord and Savior. They were not just the emotional storms and sweeping ardors of men and women long dead; they did not just reveal David's stormy career. They were a window into Jesus' inner life. These prayers of Jesus in the psalms opened beyond themselves to the divine passion, to the intricate mind and pulsing heart of God. The early church heard through the syllables and rhythms of the psalms the distant speech of another voice calling them to be more than they already were.

In praying the psalms, the early church could enter into Christ's own prayer and allow it to permeate and to transform their own being into Christ's likeness. No wonder Paul and Silas sang psalms as they spent the night in jail (Acts 16:25). How else could they express their experience of humiliation as akin to that of Christ? How else could they voice their hope of release and vindication as a victory already assured them in Christ's own ascent from the pit? The psalms, as the prayers of Jesus, put before them an example through which they could make sense of their own imperfectly formed and shadowy network of intuitions, dreams, and passions.

The psalms transformed their broken, random thoughts into a seamless fabric of being, a silver moon lying softly upon a calm pond.

Paul could sing the psalms because he had found in them an open door into the sacred. Through that door he saw a vision of the One whose power braced him up and steeled him to endure all things. He could therefore admonish the church at Ephesus:

> Therefore do not be foolish, but understand what the will of the Lord is. And do not get drunk with wine, for that is debauchery; but be filled with the Spirit, addressing one another in psalms and hymns and spiritual songs, singing and making melody to the Lord with all your heart, always and for everything giving thanks in the name of our Lord Jesus Christ to God the Father.
> —Ephesians 5:17–20, RSV

In singing and making melody with the psalms, Paul affirms that we are filled with the same spirit that animates the psalms when we sing. Filled with that mind and spirit of Christ, we no longer wander dreamily in the dark caverns of our own shadowy life. We are seized by the vision of being that rests beyond the words and rhythms of language. Our old, false self is shattered. Our true identity, the self that is our true self, bobs up and down upon the calm surface of the mind.

Paul elsewhere hints at the psalm's re-creative role. It is a unique and crucial role in our attainment of who we are meant to be and already are before God. The psalms shepherd us toward that moment when we "have put off the old nature with its practices and have put on the new nature, which is being renewed in knowledge after the image of its creator" (Col. 3:9b–10, RSV).

This moment of renewal after the image of Christ, Paul contends, is the whole aim of the Christian life. Christian life is a participation in the very life of Christ. In our baptism we die to our old, false self and are clothed in our new self. This new self is nothing less than Christ. We become a new creation. Having put to death the Old Adam, we are renewed according to the image of Christ, the New Adam (Rom. 5:12–21). Our lives conform to the pattern of Christ's descent and ascent.

> But if we have died with Christ, we believe that we shall also live with him. . . . So you also must consider yourselves dead to sin and alive to God in Christ Jesus.
> —Romans 6:8, 11, RSV

When Christ who is our life appears, then we also will appear with him in glory.

Paul pursues this conformity of our lives to the life of Christ through a multitude of images and metaphors. Our delicate faith is woven into the fabric of Christ's own warp and woof. For Paul, the expression *in Christ* or *in the Spirit* sums up our growing into conformity with the divine image. "It is no longer I who live, but Christ who lives in me" (Gal. 2:20, RSV). Paul sends the slave, Onesimus, back to his master, Philemon, "no longer as a slave but more than a slave, as a beloved brother, especially to me but how much more to you, both in the flesh and in the Lord" (Philem. 16, RSV).

> It is also called a life "in Christ," and this expression too points to the divine grace, for it is as if the pattern of existence manifested in Christ has seized the disciple and is molding his existence; this is not an external "imitation" of Christ but rather, in Bonhoeffer's language, a "conformation" of the Christian to Christ.[1]

Paul can protest, "Not I . . . but the grace of God." We are God's workmanship, created in Christ Jesus for good works (Eph. 2:10).

This life in Christ has a dual nature. It already is; but it also has a "not yet" duality. Our daily life quickly teaches us that the Spirit-filled life is not an accomplished fact. It is rather a becoming. It is a difficult and arduous task to live in Christ. Despite our having taken root in the New Adam, parts of our being remain mired down in the old creation, muddy and bespattered. We are, says Paul, born in sin. We always remain somewhat under the sign of contradiction.

The psalms have a part to play in this growing life "in

Christ." They guide us toward that moment when our false self is shattered, and we realize who we truly are. They also bring focus and direction to that arduous task of becoming, which is so much a part of the Christian life.

The false identity that the psalms help to expose is the persistent and invincible illusion of the *self*, which lies at the heart of our broken existence. This illusion is the source of our endless and futile desires. It ties us to the old creation. The image of the living God, which has been impressed upon us, suffers distortion from the moment of our birth. This deepest self is so delicate and elusive that we often fail even to discern its existence. Because it is at the core of our perceiving and experiencing, it can never become an object of our experience. Hence, we often fail to discern its reality. As our true subjectivity, it cannot sense itself as an object. Although it subsists in us, we cannot transform it into something we then observe. Annie Dillard describes movingly this elusiveness of the true self in her *Pilgrim at Tinker Creek*. Dillard has stopped along a mountain road to drink her coffee and pet a dog. She smells the loam on the wind. She pats the puppy. She watches the mountain.

> Shadows lope along the mountain's rumpled flanks; they elongate like root tips, like lobes of spilling water, faster and faster. A warm purple pigment pools in each ruck and tuck of the rock; it deepens and spreads, boring crevasses, canyons. As the purple vaults and slides, it tricks out the unleafed forest and rumpled rock in gilt, in shape-shifting patches of glow. These gold lights veer and retract, shatter and glide in a series of dazzling splashes, shrinking, leaking, exploding. . . . The air cools; the puppy's skin is hot. I am more alive than all the world.
>
> This is it, I think, this is it, right now, the present. . . . And the second I verbalize this awareness in my brain, I cease to see the mountain or feel the puppy. I am opaque, so much black asphalt.[2]

Our deep self subsists in us and is us. The moment we begin to turn our attention to it, however, it eludes the grasp of our thoughts and destroys even our vague and fragmentary awareness of it.

Unsure of the true self's reality, we turn instead to the identity-giving structures of the false self. We attempt to assert our reality by "making like" something else. We establish our self-ness and identity by doing and achieving. Whereas the true self eludes us, the false self is observable. We can point to its achievements and say: "I did this." Our sense of self becomes grounded in our doing. The more we achieve, the more experiences we gather into ourselves, the more "real" we are. This is our deepest illusion. We believe that we can forge our own identities, that we are the collective impressions of our surroundings. We convince ourselves that we are the trophies and distinctions that we have won. The false self dimly realizes that it is but a shadow, and so it convinces itself that it indeed exists because it can act, judge, discriminate.

> All sin starts from the assumption that my false self, the self that exists only in my own egocentric desires, is the fundamental reality of life to which everything else in the universe is ordered. Thus I use up my life in the desire for pleasures and the thirst for experiences, for power, honor, knowledge and love, to clothe this false self and construct its nothingness into something objectively real. And I wind experiences around myself and cover myself with pleasures and glory like bandages in order to make myself perceptible to myself and to the world, as if I were an invisible body that could only become visible when something visible covered its surface.[3]

The self's reality becomes defined in functional categories rather than categories of being.

Even more insidious is the tendency to become other-directed. It is bad enough to become a prisoner to our own false ego's necessities. It is still worse to judge the value of even this functioning and doing so solely upon how others perceive, value, and judge it. We postpone valuing even our own doing in order to see how the audience is reacting.

Our false self's quest for proof of its reality is a flesh-eating bird, Thomas Merton's "birds of appetite," which descend upon any achievement or experience that they believe will satiate their endless hunger. The hunger remains, however, because the false self, being false, cannot ever secure the tokens of true being that it pursues.

Certain philosophical and technical developments within our cultural tradition have made even more destructive this innate human tendency. Our thinking, measuring, estimating, observing is our primary reality. The more we are able to analyze and observe objects, the more we can manipulate things for our own advantage; the more these objects can be controlled, the more alive and real we are. The consequence of this activity is that we, enclosed in our bubbles of self-consciousness, become increasingly detached and isolated from everything about us and within us. Alienated from both the inside and the outside worlds, the individual self senses an acute loneliness that it no longer knows how to overcome.

As a consequence of this division, most of us are aware of ourselves as isolated egos existing inside bodies. "The mind has been separated from the body and given the futile task of controlling it, thus causing an apparent conflict between the conscious will and the involuntary instincts."[4] We are then further split into a large number of separate compartments and boxes. All our activities, talents, feelings, and emotions are set against each other in endless conflicts. This inner fragmentation breeds a fragmentation of the outside world, which is seen as a multitude of separate objects and events. The natural world is treated as if it consisted of so many chunks of water, air, soil, or minerals to be exploited by different interest groups. This inner fragmentation leads to our viewing society as split into different races, classes, political groups, or nations in competition with each other. "The belief that all these fragments—in ourselves, in our environment and in our society—are really separate can be seen as the essential reason for the present series of social, ecological and cultural crises."[5]

This philosophical and technical revolution has brought a quantum leap in our knowledge and our ability to manipulate our world. It has freed us from many of the plagues and ills that afflicted earlier generations. It has, on the other hand, introduced a far more threatening set of perils. While our lives may be less oppressive than those of our predecessors, they are fraught with far more destructive risks.

Our attitudes and perceptions of the world threaten to enclose us ever more tightly within Weber's iron cage. The distinctions between living things and inanimate objects becomes more and more blurred. We speak of "generations" and "families" of missiles. Economists ascribe to our economic fluctuations a lawfulness analogous to the cycles of nature. The result is that more and more people feel that they are victims of inhuman and ungodly chance. Industrial society's attempt "to identify with the machine as if it were a new totem animal leads ... into a self-perpetuating race for robot-like efficiency, and yet also to the question as to what, when all adjustments are made, is left of a human 'identity.' "[6]

Our false self, having "made like" the machines and computers that surround it, has snapped the slender threads that yet linked it to deeper realities. Severed from the world of meaning within and the natural world without, the false self has spun out its own equally false universe. So blind has it become to its wellsprings of being, that this artificial and alienated self threatens now to obliterate in nuclear conflagration or in toxic chemical pollution the very dimensions of being that sustain it.

Unlike the lower creatures that are locked safely within their particular natures, human beings possess freedom. We can, as Loren Eiseley states so forcefully, define and redefine our own humanity, our own conception of ourselves. In so doing, we "may give wings to the spirit or reshape [ourselves] into something more genuinely bestial than any beast of prey obeying its own nature." In this ability to take on the shape of our own dreams, we extend "beyond visible nature into another and stranger realm."[7] While we are bound through our bodies to this natural world of time and space, our minds spin out another world, a world both of possible delights and frightening terrors. These two worlds, nature and human consciousness, still maintain a precarious balance. This is, however, only temporary. "Into one or the other or into a terrifying nothing one of these two worlds must finally subside."[8]

Our overwhelming sense of guilt is another consequence of this false self. Our achieving is put into the service of something that is not real, not true to our best self. We feel, consequently, a vague sense of having betrayed the true and real within us.

Only crucifixion of our false self, which often reduces other things to objects for our enlightenment and satisfaction, can heal us of our alienation and guilt. We live in a culture that thrives on the exploitation of this false self's desire for self-satisfaction and self-authentication. This is the Faustian bargain: to sell the soul for objective knowledge deprived of wisdom. From this Faustian and false culture we must somehow seek liberation. We must crucify our knowledge in order that we might find true wisdom. Satan appears in the Genesis narratives as the one who proffers humanity *knowledge* of good and evil. Job's friends bring as their consolation *knowledge* about life's ways. The realm of objective knowledge is a perilous place in which humanity is subject to the demonic. When informed by wisdom, however, knowledge is tamed. Paul distinguished in First Corinthians 1 and 2 between rational knowledge of words and things and a wisdom that goes beyond knowledge to embrace paradox and mystery. Only when one is liberated from the knowledge of objective speech can one attain true wisdom of self. This process involves crucifixion and resurrection. "The word of the Cross," Merton declares, is this "stark and existential experience of union with Christ in His death in order to share in His resurrection."[9] It is being nailed to the cross with Christ "so that the ego-self is no longer the principle of our deepest actions, which now proceed from Christ living in us."[10]

As long as mere knowledge fills us, we have no room for the emptiness of wisdom. Only when our minds have become empty can they become full. We become poor in concepts that we might be rich in consciousness. Paul speaks of this self-emptying:

Have this mind among yourselves, which is yours in Christ Jesus, who, though he was in the form of God, did not count equality with God a thing to be grasped, but emptied himself, taking the form of a servant, being born in the likeness of men. And being found in human form he humbled himself and became obedient unto death, even death on a cross. Therefore God has highly exalted him and bestowed on him the name which is above every name.

—Philippians 2:5–10, RSV

This dying and rising with Christ is not the destruction of our personality; it is the dissipation of an illusion. It is the rediscovery of what we always were by virtue of being in the image of God. It is the regeneration of our consciousness. For consciousness is just experience. Knowledge is a compound of experience, understanding, and judging. Consciousness is seeing, hearing, smelling, tasting, touching. It is not inquiry, insight, formulating. It is not reflecting, marshalling, weighing the evidence. It is not making judgments of fact or possibility. It does not deliberate, decide. It is the dynamic state of being aware without knowing one is aware. It is an experience of mystery.[11] The wisdom that comes to us in this mystery is not knowledge of God or of ourselves as an object for scrutiny. It is a wisdom that informs us of our utter dependency upon God's saving and merciful care for us. Our only response is that of praise.

Commenting on the Beatitudes, Meister Eckhart writes:

I have said before that one is a poor person who does not even will to fulfill God's will, that is, who so lives that he or she is empty both of his own will and of God's will. . . . Second, we have said one is a poor person who himself understands nothing of God's activity in him or her. When one stands as free of understanding and knowing [as God stands void of all things], then that is the purest poverty. . . . People must be so empty of all things and all works, whether inward or outward, that they can become a proper home for God, wherein God may operate.[12]

God is gracious and wishes to bestow upon us life's blessings. But God can only act within God's self. So long as we retain a place within us where we expect God to act, where we attempt to manipulate God into acting, where we attempt to control what God does there, then we have locked God out. To be empty of all things and objects is to be full of God; and to be full of objects is to be empty of God. This letting go of experiences and objects is the destruction of our false self that hides behind these things. The person who has learned to let go is the one without objects in his or her life; even life itself is no longer an object.

Our true self is inclusive of all being. Our false self tries to possess reality as an object, to clutch at a certain quality or experience. In so doing it closes itself off to all the other infinite possibilities that encompass it. When the false collapses, we recognize we are no-thing and therefore are everything. When we grasp at possessing "some thing," that something keeps all the other possibilities from becoming reality. There is a "no-thing" that is not "nothing." Nothing is a blank. No-thing is the reservoir of potentiality from which all life bubbles forth. It is the source of inexhaustible possibilities. It is the *I* that experiences the *me*. Once we have relinquished all the achievements, functions, and deeds that we think constitute us, then we are free to enter into the no-thingness where we touch upon all the shimmering patterns of possibility and suggestion.[13]

There is a Zen story in which a university professor came to the Zen master Nan-in to inquire about Zen teachings. The master brought out teacups and a pot of tea. "He poured his visitor's cup full and then kept on pouring. The professor watched the overflow until he no longer could restrain himself. 'It is overfull. No more will go in!' 'Like this cup,' Nan-in said, 'you are full of your own opinions and speculations. How can I show you Zen unless you first empty your cup?'"[14]

John of the Cross wrote:

In order to arrive at having pleasure in everything,
Desire to have pleasure in nothing.
In order to arrive at possessing everything,

Desire to possess nothing.
  In order to arrive at being everything,
Desire to be nothing.
  In order to arrive at knowing everything,
Desire to know nothing.
  In order to arrive at that wherein thou has no pleasure,
Thou must go by a way wherein thou hast no pleasure.
  In order to arrive at that which thou knowest not,
Thou must go by a way that thou knowest not.

. . . .

  In order to arrive at that which thou art not, Thou must
go through that which thou art not.[15]

This negative path to God, as it is often called, assumes
that one must progressively strip off layer after layer of
the egocentric, false self until one finally arrives at the
true self, which is the living image of God within us.

While this path ultimately lies beyond all words and
speech, all movement and action, it must inevitably pass
through the words and speech of the Psalter. The psalms,
with their complex patterns of death and resurrection,
dying and rising, descent and ascent, point to that moment when our true self reveals itself amid the shattered
remains of a dying false self.

Questions for Reflection/Discussion

1. Take a few minutes in silence to think about what we call *success*. What are some of the commonly accepted characteristics of success? How does the life of Jesus compare with this notion of success?

2. Do you feel you sometimes try to live by a set of false values? What are your true values? How do you determine what is worthwhile to which to commit yourself?

3. How do you think we might be able to identify when we are being *other*-directed rather than being *inner*-directed? How can we prevent our self-worth from being defined by what others think of us? What part might the psalms play in this process?

4. If you are part of a group, find a partner and share as much of your reflections on these questions as you are comfortable sharing with one another. If you are studying on your own, you may find it helpful to record your reflections in a journal.

CHAPTER SIX: *Giving Shape to Formless Yearnings*

THE PSALMS ARE a verbal representation of Jesus' death and resurrection. This crucified Christ is the center of all Christian thought and life. The rivulets of the New Testament come together in the crucifixion and resurrection. They then flow out again from it. In the psalms, the early communities of Christ found a manifestation of Jesus' inner heart and mind as he moved toward, through, and beyond his passion. The psalms could carry this meaning because they expressed the emotions of those individuals who had likewise been driven to the boundaries of life by experiences of painful dislocation and unexpected relocation. Jesus first turned to these impassioned songs and prayers because they alone could contain and render coherent his own painful sorrow and anxious fear. The church later turned to them as the prayers of Jesus and as an entry into the divine being.

The psalms as the prayers of Jesus could give the early church focus and a pattern for their own experiences of dislocation and gracious relocation. The psalms were a representation of Jesus' inner history. What was enacted in baptism could be spoken over and over in the psalms. What was physically done in baptism could be mediated and internalized through the psalms. By means of the psalms, the Christian could draw the false self down into the spiraling vortex of relinquishment. At last that false self would be shattered upon the "word of the cross." In one sense this word of the cross is quite literally a *word*. It is the verbal word and image embedded in the Psalter. Pursuing these same metaphors and symbols back upward, the one who recited the psalms could share in Jesus' elation and Easter joy. He or she could experience life as sheer gift. The revealing power of the psalms enabled the self to experience its essential poverty and nakedness, which the false self desperately seeks to cloak and to forget in a shroud of achievements and experiences.

Certain situations tend to crack the hard, defensive shell of the false self. These human moments contain a certain ultimate limit or horizon beyond which the false self cannot manipulate and control. Two kinds of such limiting horizons exist: either those boundary situations of guilt, anxiety, sickness and recognition of death; or those ecstatic situations of intense joy, love, reassurance, or creation. These are precisely the experiences examined by the psalms. To pray the psalms is to meditate upon those moments that our false self least wants to face. This contemplation potentially requires us to recognize the limiting false self for what it really is and then to acknowledge our lives as ecstatic—from beyond ourselves.

Paul Tillich speaks of "boundary situations" as essential to our awakening.

> This is the dialectic of existence; each of life's possibilities drives of its own accord to a boundary and beyond the boundary where it meets that which limits it. The [person] who stands on many boundaries experiences the unrest, insecurity, and inner limitation of existence. . . . knows the impossibility of attaining serenity, security, and perfection.[1]

When the announcement of serious illness is made, we begin to experience the everyday world as suddenly rather unreal and foreign to the now suddenly real world within us. The false self has reached a limit of experience it cannot control or manipulate. Its own basic unreality, as well as the false world it has spun out of its own dream life, is revealed and exposed. The self-and-other transcendence of authentic love puts us in touch with this same dimension of being, which rests beyond the false self's world. For that single moment we are beyond ourselves and experience ourselves as surrounded by a world of infinite grace and possibility, a world far richer and more profound than our own self-limited and self-limiting false self.

David Tracy suggests that reflection upon these limit

experiences discloses the reality of another dimension of being in the world:

> a dimension whose first key is its reality as limit-to our other everyday, moral, scientific, cultural, and political activities; a dimension which, in my own brief and hazy glimpses, discloses a reality, however named and in whatever manner experienced, which functions as a final, now gracious, now frightening, now trustworthy, now absurd, always uncontrollable limit-of the very meaning of existence itself. I find that, although religiously rather "unmusical" myself, I cannot deny this reality.[2]

When forced beyond the limits of our own false self, we experience the raw stuff of human life. The psalms give eloquent testimony to this. Jesus' life and death are examples of such limit experiences. Indeed, the Christian affirmation is that Jesus is the example for all genuine human existence.

Jesus had no achievements to confirm his personal identity. His self could clothe itself in no accomplishments by which to say "because of this, I am real." No audience of onlookers authenticated his true self. He was alone on the cross. He was despised and rejected. He had no form or beauty. People hid their faces from him and esteemed him not (Isaiah 53). In his passion Jesus had no consolation, no companions, no guardian angels, no guiding star, no Father in heaven. No longer did he even savor his own love. No longer did he feel any spark of enthusiasm for his own proclamation but rather remained silent before his persecutors. His heart gave out. Utter helplessness overcame him.

> God's merciful hand no longer sustained him. His countenance was hidden during the passion, and Christ gaped into the darkness of nothingness and abandonment where God was no longer present.

> The Son of Man reached his destiny, stretched taut between a despising earth that had rejected him and a faceless heaven thundering God's "no" to sinful mankind.[3]

Jesus was utterly poor. This is the poverty that Eckhart commends: a poverty so complete that one is empty even of God. "For when God finds a person as poor as this, God operates his own work and a person sustains God in him, and God is himself the place of his operation, since God is an agent who acts within himself."[4] Out of this no-thingness Jesus emerges as the possessor of unlimited potentiality. He had refused to adopt a false self and conform to those around him. His unswerving allegiance to his true self brought crucifixion. It was, at the same time, the ground of his resurrection.

The psalms trace upon the delicate web of our hearts Jesus as an example for this descent into poverty of spirit. In baptism we descend into Christ's death and rise as a new creation. Baptism is a physical symbol of the false self's extinction in the boundary situation. The baptismal waters, however, have a double significance. They are at once tomb and womb. They are the watery pit of chaos and decay and the fruitful waters of no-thingness. The psalms reveal this descent and ascent of the self. They shepherd the Christian through a powerful repetition of Jesus' extinction and rebirth. The language and metaphors of the psalms address us and reshape us. They teach us to recognize the fissures of the false self and direct us toward our re-creation in the waters of no-thingness or our true self.

Our first encounter with our true self may come through this language event. Our baptism is a later and outward symbolization of this prior inner transformation. For the encounter with God, Paul affirms, is primarily a speech event.

> But how are men to call upon him in whom they have not believed? And how are they to believe in him of whom they have never heard? And how are they to hear without a preacher? And how can men preach unless they are sent? . . . So faith comes from what is heard, and what is heard comes by the preaching of Christ.
> —Romans 10:14–15a, 17, RSV

In praying the psalms as the prayer of Jesus, we bring together our inner lives with Jesus' inner life. We let our inner self be shaped by Christ's own personal history, by his poverty of spirit, by his true self. The psalms use evocative language. Their language "*evokes* to being what is not until it has been spoken."[5] Our work in praying the psalms "is somehow to bring the *stylized, disciplined speech* of the psalms together with the *raw, ragged, mostly formless experience* in our lives."[6] Praying the psalms trains us to sense within our own inner history these same movements toward utter poverty and new birth. They illuminate those dimensions of our being that will potentially crack open and shatter the false self, which we so frequently take for granted as the only self.

Paul discusses this same evocative function of the psalms in Second Corinthians 4:13–15. "Since we have the same spirit of faith as he had who wrote, 'I believed, and so I spoke,' we too believe, and so we speak, knowing that he who raised the Lord Jesus will raise us also with Jesus" (RSV). Paul draws two analogies in this passage. Both relate to the individual Christian's conformity to the dying/rising pattern of Jesus' life. The first deals with our baptism: "He who raised the Lord Jesus will raise us also with Jesus." Our true identity emerges out of the waters of potentiality after we have drowned the old, false self. The second analogy turns upon the speech-event of the psalms: "We have the same spirit of faith as he had who wrote, 'I believed, and so I spoke,' we too believe, and so we speak." Paul is here citing Psalm 116:19. He seems to be arguing that we conform our spirit to Christ's spirit by making our voice one with Christ's voice. Our praying the psalms as Christ's prayers evokes from our deepest self that same identity and mind that Christ discovered in them.

Athanasius, that tough and determined defender of the orthodox faith during the Arian controversy, advances a very similar argument in his *Letter to Marcellinus*. Athanasius has been asked by Marcellinus to explain why the psalms are so important to a monk. Athanasius compares the psalms to other books within the canon and finally concludes that the Psalter "has a certain grace of its own, and a distinctive exactitude of expression." In the other books one hears what one must do or what others have said or written about the Messiah. One listens to the prophets only as voices from the past who have something to tell us about the Messiah. The Psalter, however, "contains even the emotions of each soul, and it has the changes and rectifications of these delineated and regulated in itself." When the Christian recites the psalms he "comprehends and is taught in it the emotions of the soul, and, consequently, on the basis of that which affects him and by which he is constrained, he also is enabled by this book to possess the image deriving from the words."

In other books, one marvels at the deeds of the prophets, apostles, or the savior; but those who read always "consider themselves to be other than those about whom the passage speaks, so that they only come to the imitation of the deeds that are told to the extent that they marvel at them and desire to emulate them." By contrast, as the Christian recites the psalms, he or she recognizes these words "as being his own words. And the one who hears is deeply moved, as though he himself were speaking, and is affected by the words of the songs, as if they were his own songs."[7] The psalms introduce us to our conformity to Christ rather than presenting him for imitation. They enter into and take control of us; they guide us down to the limits where we recognize our false self in all its unreality. The psalms refuse to allow our false self to control and manipulate them as it often can do with the more objective portions of scripture.

Paul and Athanasius demonstrate that the psalms cannot be turned into objects for the false self to objectify and to study. They are not prophecies we can manipulate, parables we can think about, deeds and actions we can reflect upon. The psalms resist the false self's persistent objectification. They teach us the emotions of our own true self, which is identical to Jesus' true self. Through the psalms the Spirit of God constrains and possesses us. The psalms direct and regulate our inner life in such a way that we are brought to the boundaries of life and confronted with the self that is our true self. We discover there that everything is gift. We learn to expect nothing out of everything and everything out of nothing. This is accomplished not by our moral effort or mental concentration; it is sheer gift.

> I sing your praises, God my King,
> I bless your name for ever and ever,
> blessing you day after day,
> and praising your name for ever and ever. . . .
>
> Always true to his promises,
> Yahweh shows love in all he does.
> Only stumble, and Yahweh at once supports you,
> if others bow you down, he will raise you up.
>
> Patiently all creatures look to you
> to feed them throughout the year;
> quick to satisfy every need,
> you feed them all with a generous hand.
> —Psalm 145:1–2, 13b–16

This is the renewal of our minds that Paul speaks of in Romans 12. Once this renewal occurs, Paul affirms, all life is praise because all our life is grace.

Still more, in praying the psalms as the disciplined rhythms of other voices, we acknowledge our absolute poverty of self. We are so poor that even our voices are empty and void. This void of speech and of thought is once more Meister Eckhart's place of poverty. Our voices are dumb. Our minds are empty. Into this perfect emptiness, God enters and acts.

> Likewise the Spirit helps us in our weakness; for we do not know how to pray as we ought, but the Spirit himself intercedes for us with sighs too deep for words. And he who searches the hearts of men knows what is the mind of the Spirit, because the Spirit intercedes for the saints according to the will of God.
> —Romans 8:26–27, RSV

In praying the psalms we drink the dregs of our poverty to the lees. We discover the infinite potentiality of our deepest self as our true self.

Questions for Reflection/Discussion

1. The author states that "to pray the psalms is to meditate on those moments our false self least wants to face." Where do you find that reluctance happening for you? What psalm speaks most directly to this part of you? In what way might that psalm help give voice to your true self?

2. Why is it, do you think, that we cling so tightly to our false self and fear our true self?

3. In what ways can the psalms help us conform to the mind of Christ? How might we cooperate with that transforming power?

4. Record your reflections and insights in your journal. If you are part of a group, share those reflections and insights with your partner.

CHAPTER SEVEN: *Unlocking the Storehouse of Forgotten Possibilities*

IF WE WERE to leave the modern road that passes through Saint Neots on its way to Stilton and Peterborough, England, and to wander across the fields, we would eventually come to a quiet country church standing in the corner of a pasture with tall trees overshadowing it. Around this medieval chapel is a tiny churchyard. Before the church door is a simple tomb, effaced of every identifying mark. This is all that remains of an incredibly productive and creative experiment in Christian living.

For nearly twenty years an extended family, living together according to a rule of prayer and work, provided Christian education for neighboring children, produced a remarkable series of concordances and bound books, and translated into English a number of foreign devotional and scholarly books. Charles I, hard pressed by deteriorating relationships between the Stuart monarchy and the people, came here for rest and refuge. Richard Crashaw and George Herbert, two brilliant metaphysical poets of seventeenth-century England, drew inspiration from this place. As he lay on his deathbed, George Herbert ordered that his final poetic manuscript be sent to Nicholas Ferrar of Little Gidding.

T. S. Eliot also drew inspiration from this remote experiment of Nicholas Ferrar in Huntingdonshire when he wrote in "Little Gidding" in his *Four Quartets*:

> If you came this way,
> Taking the route you would be likely to take
> From the place you would be likely to come from,
> If you came this way in may time, you would find the hedges
> White again, in May, with voluptuary sweetness.

It would be the same at the end of the journey,
If you came at night like a broken king,

. . . .

If you came by day not knowing what you came for,
It would be the same, when you leave the rough road
And turn behind the pig-sty to the dull facade
And the tombstone. And what you thought you came for
Is only a shell, a husk of meaning

. . . .

You are not here to verify,
Instruct yourself, or inform curiosity
Or carry report. You are here to kneel
Where prayer has been valid. And prayer is more
Than an order of words, the conscious occupation
Of the praying mind, or the sound of the voice praying.[1]

What fueled this community at Little Gidding? What kindled its vision as a place of prayer and contemplation in a turbulent time?

Nicholas Ferrar had been born the son of a wealthy London merchant and had received the best Cambridge education. He had before him a career of power and influence. Ferrar had been deeply involved in the negotiations between the Virginia Company and the Privy Council concerning the status of the company charter. His conduct and abilities had so impressed the king that Ferrar was offered the opportunity to become a clerk with either the English embassy in Savoy or the Privy Council itself. With potential power and wealth before him, Ferrar suddenly turned away and retired for the rest of his life to the remote estate of Little Gidding.

He attempted to live there a Christian life within an extended family according to the principles of the Church of England. Ferrar's vision was to adopt a rule that would allow for the praise of God in the midst of family rather than monastic life. The core of his rule was the Psalter. Throughout the day the family would gather together for brief devotional offices. First they would recite psalms antiphonally; then they would read from the gospels;

finally they would join in singing a hymn. Beginning at six o'clock in the morning, they would gather for these offices fifteen times daily, ending at eight o'clock in the evening. Some years later Ferrar instituted a set of night watches from between nine o'clock in the evening and one o'clock in the morning. In this four-hour watch, the entire Psalter would be recited a second time. Thus in every twenty-four-hour period the community at Little Gidding recited the entire Psalter twice. Psalms were so central to life at Little Gidding that those children who arrived every Sunday morning half-past nine for Sunday school were called the "Psalm-children." For every new psalm that a child memorized, the Ferrars would reward that child with a prize of one penny.[2]

No aspect of life was untouched by the psalms. Through contact with the Psalter the deepest wellsprings of the human spirit were released and allowed to gush forth with their hidden treasures. Those who lived and visited at Little Gidding were virtually drenched in the rhythms and symbols of the psalms. Their lives were saturated with the Psalter. Out of this deep experience of the psalms came incredible productivity and power. In a historical period of intense conflict, political and economic instability, and spiritual ferment, Little Gidding was anchored in the emotional strength of the psalms.

Such has always been the case within the church's life and history. Dietrich Bonhoeffer, imprisoned at Finkenwalde, prayed the Psalter because it was for him a "great school of prayer." *Psalms: The Prayer Book of the Bible* was Bonhoeffer's last published work before his death. His intention was to provide Christians with a brief handbook on prayer. In a desperate historical moment Christians need to know how to pray, he asserts. The Psalter teaches this language of prayer. His *Letters and Papers from Prison* is studded with reflections upon the psalms. During his imprisonment, Bonhoeffer turns to the psalms in order to explicate his own inner feelings. Commenting on an inscription left in his cell by a previous occupant, Bonhoeffer's response is phrased in language drawn from the psalms:

Over the door of this cell one of my predecessors here has scribbled the words "In 100 years it will all be over." That was his way of trying to overcome the feeling that time spent here is a complete blank.... "My time is in thy hand" (Psalm 31:16)—that is the Bible's answer. But there is also a question which the Bible asks, and which threatens to dominate the whole subject: "Lord, how long?" (Psalm 13).[3]

In his original preface to *Praise and Lament in the Psalms*, Claus Westermann narrates how in a time of acute distress and dislocation a people rediscovered the psalms.

Only recently, and only in those places where the church was under severe trial has the praise of God been again awakened. A collection of letters from pastors of the confessing church, which were illegally printed during the church struggle, bore the title:... *And They Praised God*....

Here and there under the heavy burden of what was happening to them, members of the congregation discovered that they were not only learning patience and self-discipline under that which had been given them to bear, but that *under* the burdens, despite all trials, they were able to praise God.[4]

Westermann confesses that his own rediscovery of the psalms and a renewed fascination with them that grew into his scholarly work began only when he picked up Luther's version of the psalms while imprisoned in Nazi Germany.

Bonhoeffer, also writing under the same pressure of events that drove Westermann to the psalms, concluded that "whenever the Psalter is abandoned, an incomparable treasure vanishes from the Christian church. With its recovery will come unsuspected power."[5] Bonhoeffer here identifies the ebb and flow of the Psalter's prominence in church history. Whenever the church has been confronted with limit situations in which it recognized its own powerlessness and dependence upon God, the psalms have surged forward to express the church's poverty and emptiness before a God who acts.

The psalms have re-emerged as an important resource

during every moment of crisis when the church has had to rethink the connection between its language and human experience, between its own self-understanding and its social and cultural context. The psalms, with their inclusive treatment of human emotion and experience, provide an often neglected storehouse of forgotten possibilities. To return to that storehouse is to explore alternatives for self-understanding. As the deposit in which the mind of Christ is hidden, the psalms enable the church to connect its own corporate life once more with the primal vision of the One who called it into being as the Body of Christ.

Nowhere is this more apparent than in the patristic era. As the church came into contact with the highly developed and cultured civilization of the Greco-Roman world, it was forced to deal in new ways with what it meant to be the church. The psalms loom large in the literature and liturgical life of this era. John Chrysostom, the fourth-century patriarch of Constantinople, reported that many monks and priests knew the psalms by heart and that frequently such knowledge was a prerequisite for ordination to the priesthood. Chrysostom's friend Palladius describes a forty-mile journey across the desert with another monk who neither ate nor drank all day, but instead continually recited fifteen psalms, Hebrews, Luke's Gospel, and Proverbs as he walked. Athanasius highly commends the psalms and declares that while most scripture speaks to us, the psalms speak for us. Athanasius expresses clearly the early church's regard for the Psalter as a storehouse of alternative identities. He compares it to a garden where, because all varieties of prayer grow all year, Christians can pick freely according to their needs at any time.

Amid the urban unrest and the heretical tendencies of thirteenth-century Italy, the psalms were once again recognized as an important resource. St. Francis of Assisi modeled his "Canticle of Brother Sun" upon Psalm 148. Written at San Damiano while Francis was regaining his health in 1225, the "Canticle of Brother Sun" was probably meant to be sung by the friars as they went about their preaching tours of the villages and cities. Despite its simple lines, it is a highly complex work that echoes the themes of Psalm 148.

> Most high, omnipotent, good Lord
> To you alone belong praise and glory
> Honor, and blessing.
> No man is worthy to breathe thy name.
>
> Be praised, my Lord, for all your creatures.
>
> In the first place for the blessed Brother Sun
> who gives us the day and enlightens us through you.
> He is beautiful and radiant with his great spendor,
> Giving witness of thee, most omnipotent One.
>
> Be praised, my Lord, for Sister Moon and the stars
> Formed by you so bright, precious, and beautiful.
>
> Be praised, my Lord, for Brother Wind
> And the airy skies, so cloudy and serene;
> For every weather, be praised, for it is life-giving.
>
> Be praised, my Lord, for Sister Water
> So necessary yet so humble, precious, and chaste.
>
> Be praised, my Lord, for Brother Fire,
> Who lights up the night,
> He is beautiful and carefree, robust and fierce.
>
> Be praised, my Lord, for our sister, Mother Earth,
> who nourishes and watches us
> while bringing forth abundant fruits and colored flowers
>   and herbs.

Later in the same year Francis was able to reconcile the bishop and the mayor of Assisi who had been feuding. In celebration of that reconciliation Francis added an additional verse.

> Be praised, my Lord, for those who pardon through your
>   love
> And bear witness and trial.
> Blessed are those who endure in peace
> For they will be crowned by you, Most High.

Spending his last days in the care of Bishop Guido of Assisi, Francis composed the final verses at the episcopal residence.

> Be praised, My Lord, for our sister, bodily death,
> Whom no living man can escape.
> Woe to those who die in sin.
>
> Blessed are those who discover thy holy will.
> The second death will do them no harm.
>
> Praise and bless the Lord.
> Render him thanks.
> Serve him with great humility. Amen.[6]

In these verses we see a spirit deeply imbued with the psalms. Not only does the form depend upon Psalm 148 but also the very content of the canticle is permeated with the emotions of the psalms. It reveals a person who has descended into no-thingness and discovered that the "second death" can do no harm. Francis understands the rhythms of life as sheer grace and gift to which the only adequate response is praise. His "Canticle of Brother Sun" along with the more famous "Prayer of St. Francis" reveal a life shaped and formed by immersion in the imagery and rhythms of the psalms.

As the medieval world slowly collapsed under the pressure of the growing scientific discoveries, the exploration of the non-European world, and the economic shifts then occurring, the church once again found itself having to rethink its self-understanding. The gap between its language and human experience had grown too wide to be patched over. A massive readjustment of Christian thought and language was painfully undertaken. This shift culminated in the new understandings of the Reformation and Counter-Reformation period.

In A.D. 1415, John Huss was condemned to death by the Council of Constance. As he ascended to the stake, Huss recited Psalm 31. In 1416, one year after Huss's death, Jerome of Prague perished at the same spot while singing the same Psalm 31. In 1498, Savonarola lay near death in his cell. He had been mutilated, but his right hand had been left undamaged so that he could write a confession of conformity to his ecclesiastical authorities. He used instead that undamaged hand to compose a meditation upon the words of Psalm 31. During the same period he also wrote a second meditation on Psalm 51.[7]

The psalms gave expression to Huss, Jerome of Prague, and Savonarola. Psalm 31 in particular gave voice to their determination to trust steadfastly in God despite their impending deaths.

> In you, Yahweh, I take shelter;
> never let me be disgraced.
> In your righteousness deliver me, rescue me,
> turn your ear to me, make haste!
>
> But I put my trust in you, Yahweh,
>   I say, "You are my God."
> My days are in your hand, rescue me
>   from the hands of my enemies and persecutors;
> let your face smile on your servant,
>   save me in your love.
>
> Blessed be Yahweh, who performs
>   marvels of love for me
>   (in a fortress-city)!
> In my alarm I exclaimed,
>   "I have been snatched out of your sight!"
> Yet you heard my petition
>   when I called to you for help.
>
> Love Yahweh, all you devout:
>   Yahweh, protector of the faithful,
> will repay the arrogant
>   with interest.
> Be strong, let your heart be bold
>   all you who hope in Yahweh!
>   —Psalm 31:1–2, 14–16, 21–24

Having been shaped by the psalms, they could faithfully wait in poverty and emptiness for God's action rather than haughtily attempt to justify by achievement or by words their own lives. The psalms gave meaning to their "boundary" experience and enabled them to understand that experience of the limits in the light of Christ. No other prayers than the prayers of Jesus would suffice in their crises.

The psalms also played a prominent part in the lives of many Reformation figures such as Thomas More and John Calvin. More repeated Psalm 51:1 as he awaited execution under Henry VIII. "Have mercy on me, O God, according to thy steadfast love; according to thy abundant mercy blot out my transgressions" (RSV). The religious dissidents who populated the Massachusetts Bay Colony may have envisioned Boston as a "city set on a hill," but they named Salem, Massachusetts, after a phrase in Psalm 76: "At Salem, in his tabernacle." The *Bay Psalm Book* was the first volume printed in English North America (1640). Early Calvinists composed new metric versions of the psalms. Congregations in France and elsewhere rediscovered the singing of the Psalter. Calvin's enthusiasm for the psalms sprang from his perception of their role in Christian formation, an insight not unrelated to that of Athanasius. The psalms are, said Calvin,

> the anatomy of all the parts of the soul, for not an affection will anyone find in himself whose image is not reflected in this mirror. All the griefs, sorrows, fears, misgivings, hopes, cares, anxieties, in short all the disquieting emotions with which the minds of men are wont to be agitated, the Holy Spirit hath here pictured exactly.[8]

Both Athanasius and Calvin lived and ministered in radically unsettled times. These were boundary periods in history. Huss, Jerome of Prague, and Savonarola lived likewise in times of social, economic, and religious upheaval. The psalms were a source of power and direction in such historical and personal moments of crisis.

John Donne expressed this same conviction. Donne is best remembered for his conceits, his erotic and sensual poems, which are the most frequently anthologized ones. Donne was, however, the author of several collections of religious poetry. He was also a fine preacher and in 1621 became Dean of St. Paul's Cathedral Church in London. Donne believed that "the Psalms are the manna of the church. "All who ate manna in the wilderness found that it tasted as if it were their favorite food. Similarly, the psalms minister instruction and satisfaction to every individual in every emergency and occasion:

> David was not only a clear prophet of Christ himself, but a prophet of every particular Christian; he foretells what I,

what any, shall do and suffer and say. And as the whole book of Psalms is (as the Spouse speaks, the name of Christ) an ointment poured out upon all sorts of sores, a balm that searches all wounds; so are there some certain psalms that are imperial psalms, that command over all affections and spread themselves over all occasions.[9]

Donne expresses exactly and with precision the function of the psalms. In them we find a mirror through which we can begin to perceive our true image. This mirror must first enable us to see through the smudged and bespattered false reflection. It directs our emotions and inner spirit to that place of emptiness and poverty, abandonment and openness. At that very place we discern our true self in that same mirror of the psalms.

Teresa of Avila tells her readers that her first experience in which she heard God speak to her personally came as she was reciting the psalms:

I was reciting the Hours, I came to the verse which says: "Justus es, Domine, and Thy judgments...." I began to think how very true this was.... Thou didst answer me, Lord, saying "Serve thou Me, and meddle not with this." This was the first word which I every heard Thee speak to me and so it made me very much afraid.[10]

Nor is this conjunction of the psalms with the crises of Christian self-identity limited to isolated personalities. The same conjunction appears in the liturgical use of the Psalter in the church's worship. In the early church the psalms played a major role in Christian worship. Psalms were sung by cantors with the people singing refrains or responses. These psalms were usually interspersed between the other scripture lessons.

A second worship setting emerged during the Arian controversy. Flavian and Diodore, two devout laypersons, began to teach psalms to the orthodox faithful in order to counter the hymns and songs of the Arians, who then enjoyed not only much popular support in Antioch but even the bishop's support as well. Companies of the faithful would gather at the graves of orthodox martyrs and join in singing the psalms. They formed two groups and sung them antiphonally. Eventually Flavian became bishop of Antioch and Diodore was elevated to bishop of Tarsus. The triumph of the orthodox position, combined with the influential positions of Flavian and Diodore, led to the spread of this antiphonal psalmody. Monastic communities rapidly adopted it. John Chrysostom introduced it into his area in the late fourth century. Ambrose, bishop of Milan and mentor of St. Augustine, ushered it into the Latin Church during approximately the same era.[11] What is of most significance, however, is that the Psalter was seen as an effective defense against the songs of the Arian heretics. In a moment of critical self-definition, the orthodox faithful turned to the Psalter in order to formulate a response. They saw in the psalms the fountainhead from which flowed the inner heart and mind of Christ. Faced with controversial and painful choices about how to understand not only who Christ is but who the Christian is, Flavian and Diodore immersed themselves and their followers in the Psalter.

A similar process occurred during the Reformation and Counter-Reformation period. The church's role and place in society was secure and unquestioned by the high Middle Ages. The more secure this identity grew, the less importance the psalms played in the church's worship. Psalms had traditionally been sung between lessons, at the offertory, and at communion. With the disappearance of processions and the decline of lay communion, only a few brief verses or a minor response remained of the lush use of the Psalter that had characterized the early church. With the Reformation came a new emphasis upon the psalms and their use in the church's worship. The reformed tradition in particular produced a new generation of psalm paraphrases set to new tunes. The Geneva Psalter of 1562 along with the Scottish Psalter of 1615 opened a new era in the church's use of the psalms that were sung at public worship and in private devotions. Christian self-understanding had once more returned to the psalms in an effort to understand what it meant to live with the mind of Christ. In a world where the old certainties and signposts had disappeared, the psalms provided protestant piety with a means of self-definition and communal exploration. The tremendous creative energy released by the protestant communities of France and Great Britain must in some way be linked to the secure self-understanding provided to a religious community grounded in the mind of Christ.

Gradually, however, the psalms were eclipsed by the popularity of sung hymns. The late eighteenth and nineteenth centuries saw an explosion of popular hymns written by poets and preachers. Many of these hymns reflected the personal and public piety of their generation and enjoyed enormous success. On my shelf is a copy of the Presbyterian hymnal of 1867. It is titled *Psalms and Hymns for the Worship of God,* and it is precisely what it says that it is. The first 166 pages are metrical psalm paraphrases. The remaining 400 pages are contemporary hymns and songs. These are arranged under various topical headings such as "time and eternity," "expostulations," "the trinity," or "receiving Christ." While the psalms still are placed at the front of the book, their numbers are far overshadowed by the popular songs and hymns.

What is more striking is the subtle message conveyed beneath the surface. The Psalter cannot be reduced to convenient and controllable categories. It defies easy objectification. The psalms, as Athanasius, Chrysostom, Teresa of Avila, and even Calvin understood, insist on shaping the hearer through the power of metaphor and language event. The hymns and songs, however, fit nicely into the rational tradition that so dominated the nineteenth century. The hymns could be selected by the worship leader to elicit the desired effect from the worshipers. If he preached on sin he could pick hymns from the section on "penitence." If she preached on virtue she could select songs from "faith," "example," or "love." The psalms, on the other hand, required the Christian to conform to their patterns, rhythms, cadences.

The twentieth century has witnessed two global wars of horrifying destructiveness. This experience, along with an increasing awareness that our scientific and technological models cannot account for all reality, has shaken our rational confidence. There is profound disquiet in the

Christian self-understanding that in some ways parallels the breakup of the older world view. Increasingly, the church speaks of living in a post-Christian world. Some Europeans speak of their culture as neo-pagan. Once again the church is confronted with what it means to be Christian in a changing world. Individual Christians are again sensitive to the gap between their language and their experience. How does the faith relate to global hunger, to the increasingly unstable political and economic structures established in this century, to newly evolved understandings of what it means to be human?

Against this background, it is not difficult to perceive why the psalms have moved to the center of Christian reflection and devotion once more. New translations and musical settings are being tested. The recovery of the Psalter for public worship and private devotion is underway. Like Flavian and Diodore, the contemporary church is discovering that the Psalter is the storehouse of forgotten possibilities. To recover the psalms as the prayerbook of Jesus is to recover the possiblilty of discovering what Christ calls the church to be in our age. Bonhoeffer's observation is even more apt today than when he scribbled it into his notes: "The psalter is an incomparable treasure and with its recovery comes unsuspected power."

Questions for Reflection/Discussion

1. Using a hymnal, compare the following hymns with the psalms that inspired them. Then reflect upon the questions that follow:

Psalm 23	"He Leadeth Me: O Blessed Thought"
Psalm 24	"Lift Up Your Heads, Ye Mighty Gates"
Psalm 46	"A Mighty Fortress Is Our God"
Psalm 90	"O God, Our Help in Ages Past"
Psalm 98	"Joy to the World"
Psalm 100	"All People That on Earth Do Dwell"
Psalm 103	"Praise to the Lord, the Almighty"
Psalm 104	"O Worship the King"
Psalm 130	"Out of the Depths I Cry to Thee"
Psalm 146	"I'll Praise My Maker While I've Breath"

2. In your opinion, how did the psalm affect the nature of the hymn?

3. Which speaks more powerfully to you—the hymn or the psalm? Why do you think this is so? To which is it easier for you to relate?

4. Why do you think the hymn writer was inspired by that particular psalm?

5. Discuss your findings with your partner or record your reflections in your journal.

CHAPTER EIGHT: *Rediscovering an Unsuspected Power*

IN THE MUSICAL version of *Don Quixote, Man of La Mancha*, Quixote enters a local inn and meets a young prostitute, Aldonza. Since Quixote sees not a mere inn but a castle, Aldonza must consequently be the lady of the manor. He calls her "Dulcinea," a verbal image of his ideal lady, instead of her everyday name of Aldonza. At first she is entranced and delighted by Quixote's attention and devotion. Then she comes to hate him because in showing her what her life might have been, he has only made what she is more unbearable. She becomes Quixote's tormentor. Their relationship, however, undergoes one more transformation. As Quixote lies dying, Aldonza and Sancho arrive to be with him. The bystanders chide her for wanting to be identified with this obviously crazy old man. When they call her Aldonza, she replies sharply, "My name is Dulcinea."

In this brief encounter meant for popular entertainment, we discover a striking illustration of the biblical concept of God's "Word." Quixote's words have had a transformative effect. Aldonza has literally become Dulcinea because of a word that Quixote has spoken to her. A "speech event" or "language event" is the sign that gives Aldonza a vision of an alternative mode of being-in-the-world.[1] Quixote's speech event presents Aldonza with another vision of reality, which she then must reject or embrace. In the end she embraces this new vision and becomes a new person. God also speaks to us in language events and presents us with new visions of reality to which we must then respond. Salvation, Paul tells the Romans, comes from hearing the proclamation of the Word (Rom. 10:14–17). To hear and to respond to the divine Word is to adopt a different mode of being in the world.

103

We generally view speech as syllables that describe objects. I say *tree* and I mean the object with green leaves and a brown trunk next to my house. These linguistic bits offer us a tool with which to manipulate and handle our inner and outer worlds. We use language to describe and thereby to objectify our emotions, other people, or even concepts. This is the descriptive function of language. It is a necessary function and one without which we could not exist as a society. There is more, however, than descriptive language. According to the biblical tradition, words are not functional tools with which to exploit reality to our own advantage. Language can make things happen. It can give reality a shape and a texture that did not previously exist. Language is creative.

Some linguistic philosophers distinguish between a *spoken word* and a *speaking word*. A spoken word is the language of descriptive speech. We speak and our words become objects among other objects. A speaking word is a word that constitutes and creates. It evokes new realities.

In "The Motive for Metaphor," Wallace Stevens explores this interaction of the spoken and the speaking word.

> You like it under the trees in autumn,
> Because everything is half dead.
> The wind moves like a cripple among the leaves
> And repeats words without meaning.
>
> In the same way, you were happy in spring,
> With the half colors of quarter-things,
> The slightly brighter sky, the melting clouds,
> The single bird, the obscure moon—
>
> The obscure moon lighting an obscure world
> Of things that would never be quite expressed,
> Where you yourself were never quite yourself
> And did not want nor have to be,
>
> Desiring the exhilarations of changes:
> The motive for metaphor, shrinking from
> The weight of primary noon,
> The A B C of being,
>
> The ruddy tempter, the hammer
> Of red and blue, the hard sound—

Steel against intimation—the sharp flash,
The vital, arrogant, fatal, dominant X.[2]

Our world of descriptive language is a heavy and sometimes oppressive one. It contains within it the weight of
primary noon that wants everything clear and objective.
It is uncomfortable with evocative language, seeking to
suppress it: "the hard sound—steel against intimation."
The spoken word cares only about "the A B C of being."
It is the dominant X. The language of imagination, however,
is a speaking word. It is not content with an obscure half
world full of well-defined quarter-things. It sweeps away
this crippled, repetitive, meaningless world and replaces
it with something new and vital.

The biblical tradition affirms that God's Word creates
the cosmos fresh every moment. It spins out new worlds
and populates them with all manner of living, creeping,
flying, and thinking creatures. God said, "Let there be
light." And there was light. "So shall my word be that
goes forth from my mouth; it shall not return to me
empty, but it shall accomplish that which I purpose, and
prosper in the thing for which I sent it" (Isa. 55:11, RSV).

The psalms hymn this speaking word under the head-
ing of "wisdom" or "Torah."

The word of Yahweh is integrity itself,
all he does is done faithfully;
he loves virtue and justice,
Yahweh's love fills the earth.

By the word of Yahweh the heavens were made,
their whole array by the breath of his mouth;
he collects the ocean waters as though in a wineskin,
he stores the deeps in cellars.

Let the whole world fear Yahweh,
let all who live on earth revere him!
He spoke, and it was created;
he commanded, and there it stood.
—Psalm 33:4–9

Since this divine Word is enfleshed in life, we can perceive dimly the traces of the divine mind in all life.

Attentive to this divine language event embedded in all reality, the psalmist calls upon his hearers to watch and to meditate upon life as the arena where God is revealed. Psalm 1 affirms that the one who meditates upon God's Word is like a tree planted by sweet waters that flourishes and bears fruit. Psalm 119, the longest psalm in the entire Psalter, is an elaborate meditation upon God's Word. The patterns of reality, it says, reveal God's torah. This Law is a "lamp to my feet and a light to my path" (Psalm 119:105, RSV).

> This poem is not, and does not pretend to be, a sudden outpouring of the heart like, say, Psalm 18. It is a pattern, a thing done like embroidery, stitch by stitch, through long, quiet hours, for love of the subject and for the delight in leisurely, disciplined craftsmanship. . . . We can guess at once that he felt about the Law somewhat as he felt about his poetry; both involved exact and loving conformity to an intricate pattern. . . . The Order of the Divine mind, embodied in the Divine Law, is beautiful.[3]

One of our time's great tragedies is that we have lost this speaking word. All that we retain is the flat and absolutizing spoken word. Our poverty of speech has smoothed down and polished away the sharp and creative moments of the language event. We have reduced our language to spoken words, descriptions, manipulations of data and information. Our speech has been stripped of power. We no longer perceive the intricate pattern, the divine order, the Word sprung fresh from the mind of God.

Loren Eiseley tells of walking along the shore of a desolate island off the Gulf Coast. He salvaged from the surf a beautiful shell, imprinted with what appeared to be strange writing. The golden letters ran in symmetrical lines around the shell's conical surface. Taking it to an antiquities dealer, Eiseley was told that it was the alphabet shell, *conus spurius atlanticus*. This, for Eiseley, was the ultimate misnomer. Only one who has totally misread nature and life could call it spurious.

The shell surely contained a message. For "we live by

messages. . Some of the messages cannot be read, but [we] will always try." We hunger for messages; and when we cease to seek and to interpret them, we will cease to be human. We "decipher from the ancient alphabets of nature only those secrets that [our] own deeps possess the power to endow with meaning. . . . The golden alphabet, in whatever shape it chooses to reveal itself, is never spurious."[4] From its inscrutable lettering we are created along with all the streaming cloudland of our dreams.

The prophet Amos spoke of a time when words would crack and sometimes break under the burden of objectification. A famine would come upon the land. Men and women would wander from sea to sea, from north to south. They would search not for bread or fresh water but for the Word of the Lord. "They shall run to and fro, to seek the word of the Lord, but they shall not find it" (Amos 8:11–12, RSV). That famine has come upon our land and upon our time. It is the famine for the speaking word, for the word that opens up new realities, for the word that creates new worlds in which we may find a more encompassing and embracing meaning for our lives.

At the fountain of the psalms we may slake our thirst and satisfy our hunger for a speaking word. Nestled in the Psalter's rhythms and rich cadences is a language event that calls into being a whole cosmos of meaning within us. The psalms speak a yet living and dynamic word. They do not provide a tool for manipulating and controlling our passions, dreams, fears, and intuitions. They do not enable us to objectify life about us into rigid and abstract frameworks. They help us relinquish the false world of our false self in order that we might discern, however dimly and distantly, the outlines of another encircling reality.

This is why the synagogue and early church alike turned to the psalms. Here was a living language. The early church could readily see in Israel's praises their own Word incarnate. Jesus, a speaking word sent from the heart of God in the fullness of time, had tented in their midst. He was a Word full of grace and truth. He was the fruition of all God's prior speaking his heart through the language events of the psalms. The Book of

Psalms, then, is not primarily a book of poetry or biography or speculation, though it contains elements of all these. It is certainly not a book of prophecy or history, though some have read it as such. It is a religious book, a book of devotion. It is a rich deposit of metaphors. The Psalter is a speaking word that contains the inherent power to interpret and to order our present world of experience.

This is why those who lived and ministered in times of crisis turned to the Psalter. It demarcated the true dimensions of their lives. They did not turn to the Psalter in order to find a spoken word that they could then manipulate into a word of comfort, prophecy, or command. They turned to the psalms so that the depths of being itself could speak its creative word to them and evoke a new quality of being from them.

Bonhoeffer described the Psalter as an incomparable treasure. When the church, he asserted, recovered the psalms, it would recover unsuspected power.[5] The church has passed through a period of rapid, radical, and irrevocable change in its theory and practice of worship. Part of this change has been the recovery of those elements of which Bonhoeffer hinted. Three generally agreed upon principles have emerged in discussions of Christian worship. Two relate directly to the psalms: recovery of the centrality of scripture and recovery of authentic praise.

The church cannot remain "Christian" without a consistent and ongoing encounter with the biblical message. The individual and corporate stories of the Christian community are shaped by the story that is revealed in scripture. Only dialogue with this biblical story enables the church to discover what it means to be the people of God.

The psalms are integral to this recovery of scripture. They provide a concise summary of the biblical history of salvation. Luther called the psalms the "Bible in miniature." The hymns of praise often summarize the themes of creation (Psalms 8, 19, 104, and 148).

> Yahweh, our Lord,
> how great is your name throughout the earth!

Above the heavens is your majesty chanted
by the mouths of children, babes in arms.
You set your stronghold firm against your foes
to subdue enemies and rebels.

I look up at your heavens, made by your fingers,
at the moon and stars you set in place—
ah, what is man that you should spare a thought for
  him,
the son of man that you should care for him?

Yet you have made him little less than a god,
you have crowned him with glory and splendor,
made him lord over the work of your hands,
set all things under his feet.
                                        —Psalm 8:1–6

Other psalms sing of Abraham's election and of God's
promises to the patriarchs. Still others reflect the Exodus,
the rebellion in the wilderness, and the conquest of the
settled land (Psalms 66:1–12, 100; 111; 114; 149; 105).

Remember his covenant for ever,
his word of command for a thousand generations,
the pact he made with Abraham,
his oath to Isaac.

He sent his servant Moses,
and Aaron, the man of his choice;
there they displayed his signs,
his wonders in the land of Ham.

They demanded food, he sent them quails,
he satisfied them with the bread of heaven;
he opened the rock, the waters gushed
to flow through the desert like a river.

He gave them the pagans' territories.
Where others had toiled, they took possession,
on condition that they kept his statutes
and remained obedient to his laws.
                —Psalm 105:8–9, 26–27, 40–41, 44–45

Still other psalms focus upon the Davidic monarch and
the fate of Israel in the time of Assyria and Babylon
(Psalms 2, 18, 20, 21, 45, 72, 78, 89, 101, 110, 132, 144).

Many of the communal laments and thanksgivings echo the suffering of Judah in exile and its longing for Zion when they were scattered among the nations.

> Bedside the streams of Babylon
> we sat and wept
> at the memory of Zion,
> leaving our harps
> hanging on the poplars there.
>
> For we had been asked
> to sing to our captors,
> to entertain those who had carried us off:
> "Sing" they said
> "some hymns of Zion."
> —Psalm 137:1–3

As the prayers of Jesus, the psalms gathered into themselves not only the broad and sweeping movements within Israel's long and varied history, but also the inner movements of Jesus' life. Into their metaphors and images the psalms received the impression of Jesus' life, death, and resurrection.

As the church recites the psalms, it learns in summary form the inner meaning of its place within God's economy of salvation. Moreover, this summary is poetic in form. Its poetic survey of the human situation is so comprehensive that all of life finds a home within it. This is, after all, the very nature of poetry as opposed to prose.

> Poetry is the most direct and simple means of expressing oneself in words: the most primitive nations have poetry, but only quite well developed civilizations can produce good prose. . . . prose is a much less natural way of speaking than poetry is.[6]

The poetry of the Psalter can tell us things about our human condition that we cannot understand in any other way. The poetic form also serves as an aid to memory. This is particularly true of Hebrew poetry. It does not possess the metrical structure of English or European poetry. It relies primarily upon meaning. Ideas and meaning play a more significant role than sound and cadence. Parallelism, the central technique of Hebrew poetry, serves to reinforce ideas and contribute to their memorable quality. Unlike other readings from scripture in worship, the psalms are not just heard by passive listeners. They engage the congregation in the recitation of scripture. A variety of techniques accomplish this: musical or spoken refrains between stanzas, antiphonal readings, unison reading, or singing of the whole psalm. This engages more than one sense of the worshiper and allows the scriptural word to be appropriated on several levels simultaneously. Athanasius already perceived this in the first centuries of the church. Athanasius already perceived this in the first centuries of the church. "Just as harmony that unites flutes effects a single sound, so also, seeing that different movements appear in the soul," the psalms unite this movement into an inner harmony. We are not meant to be discordant or at variance with ourselves. Through the psalms we become ourselves a stringed instrument and devote ourselves completely to the Spirit. Thus we come to obey in all our members and emotions and to serve in our whole person the will of God. "The harmonious reading of the Psalms is a figure and type of such undisturbed and calm equanimity of our thoughts."[7] To recover the psalms is to recover the centrality of scripture in the church's life. To recover the psalms is to rediscover the infinite riches of expression and experience within the biblical tradition.

Gathering into themselves all the themes of sin and forgiveness, grace and judgment, the psalms often offer a more balanced picture of God's interaction with humankind than the rest of scripture, which presents only its partial view. The psalms provide a bridge between the moralism that too easily condemns and the sacramentalism that too easily condones. More humanely than the prophets and more rigidly than the priests, the psalmists understood our inability to win our own salvation by obedience to a law or the use of a hallowed technique.

They offered the pastoral consolations of the priests without neglecting the moral demands of the prophets for righteousness in living. They spoke the harsh word of God's judgment without producing despair, and they conveyed the soothing benefits of religion without inducing indolence or self-arrogance.[8]

Through the psalms we hear the great chorus of the people of God who responded and are continually responding to God's presence and absence in their lives. The psalms catch us up in this same dramatic story and remind us that it is our story, our hymn of praise.

This dimension of praise is the second major discovery in contemporary worship. The recovery of praise has been a major theme in worship discussions. Praise draws into it all the emotive aspects that our rational, scientific, modern culture has often excluded and upon which it has frowned.

Praise has a bipolar structure. On the one side, it is impressive. This impressive function helps the worshiper learn the vocabulary of praise. It provides the forms and structures that the worshiper can utilize to interpret and to make coherent his or her own vague and shadowy feelings of gratitude, wonder, and awe. On the other side, praise is expressive. This function helps individuals get their feelings out. It helps the worshiper respond to the word.

Both of these aspects are in the service of a far greater purpose. In Hebrew *yadah*, "to praise," is also translated as "to confess." To praise God is to confess our belief in God's gracious care. Our ability to confess this experience is related directly to our ability to taste it ever more deeply. Our praise of God mysteriously enlarges our capacity to experience God's presence. In our giving, we are the ones who are given the gift. In our giving, we are the ones who are given the gift. It is in the process of being worshipped that God communicates the divine presence to us. "It is not of course the only way. But for many people at many times, the 'fair beauty of the Lord' is revealed chiefly or only while they worship...together."

Even in Judaism the sacrifice's essence was not that worshipers gave bulls and goats to God. Rather, God gave the divine gift of presence to them through the occasion of their own giving. Similarly, "in the central act of our own worship of course this is far clearer—there it is manifestly, even physically, God who gives and we who receive."[9]

In the eucharist, our supreme act of praise and thanksgiving, we bring our gifts and lift our voices in praise. Yet we are the ones who receive the final gift. In praising God, our capacity for experience is enlarged; our ability to perceive the movements of God's grace is expanded. We bring our gift of praise but are given the far greater gift of God's blessing in return.

This recovery of praise has a very practical impact upon our lives. The more we praise, the more we are capable of entertaining the beauty and goodness God places within and about us. Those who never have a good word to say are often those who are most unhappy in life. To praise is to "taste and see that the Lord is good" indeed. Without praise we die inwardly. Our capacity for enjoying life fades like ashes sprinkled upon the waters of a brackish stream. A seemingly unwritten law of existence is that joy and happiness are incomplete until they can be expressed in some form of praise. It is frustrating to have finished a good book and to have no one with whom to discuss its lucid prose and intricate design. If we go to a movie or symphony by ourselves we are apt to return home more lonely than we were before. Without someone with whom to share our excitement for the production, our enthusiasm is deficient and partial. Thus the Scottish catechism affirms that our chief end is to glorify God and to enjoy God forever. At first glance this seems an odd juxtaposition of ideas. What we fail to realize is that our enjoyment of God is incomplete until it is expressed in our joining with the saints in their unending glorification of God. Our savoring of life's delights is lacking so long as we cannot praise the Giver who is also the Gift.[10]

The psalms affirm this when they say that those who are dead cannot praise God. Praising is to life as not praising is to death. "Nowhere is there the possibillity of abiding, true life that does not praise God. Praise of God, like petition, is a mode of existence, not something which may or may not be present in life."[11]

Praise also grounds and roots us in our tasks that lie daily before us. We do not praise the abstract. We praise the immediate and the material. The work of evil is abstraction.

Praise calls us back to the immediate from the realm of abstraction. John Milton in *Paradise Lost* wrote:

> But apt the mind or fancy is to rove
> Uncheck'd, and of her roving is no end;
> Til warn'd, or by experience taught, she learn,
> That not to know at large of things remote
> From use, obscure and subtle, but to know
> That which before us lies in daily life,
> Is the prime wisdom; what is more, is fume,
> Or emptiness, or fond impertinence.[12]

The psalmists praise the small victories of life: recovery from illness, the birth of a child, the end of a personality conflict, the cessation of hostilities between neighbors. The grand visions of creation and redemption are there; but they are given their place only by a context that focuses first upon "that which before us lies in daily life." Praise, when rightly understood as the psalmists teach us, shifts our gaze from "at large things remote from us" to the obvious and often overlooked daily events where God so frequently is manifest.

The recovery of praise also has important social implications for the church. One cannot avoid praising something. Praise is essential to being alive. If we do not praise God, then some idol will receive our praise: an institution, an idea, a person. Failing all else, we praise only our own self. Since we die when we do not praise, something must rush in to fill the void when God is not praised. This artificial praise will sustain our lives but only at a weakened and lessened level.

There is no real existence that does not admire and praise something. For Israel, God is so real and so mighty that such honor and exaltation can be directed nowhere but to God. To direct this praise elsewhere is to undermine life itself. "If the praise of God...belongs to existence, then the directing of this praise to a man, an idea, or an institution must disturb and finally destroy life itself."[13] Our praise, then, is one dimension of our struggle for liberation from all powers and principalities that would enslave us to them. To praise God is to hurl a defiant "no" in the face of those forces that demand our absolute obedience and insist that we be willing to sacrifice everything to insure their survival. Bonhoeffer's last published book could only be upon the Psalter. To join one's voice with the psalmist's praise of God was to defy a totalitarian regime that demanded absolute obedience. This praise is not just one's individual and solitary voice but is an entire chorus of the whole people of God. "Whenever one in his enforced separation praised God in song, or speech, or silence, he was conscious of himself not as an individual, but as a member of the congregation," Westermann recalls. The praise of the worshiping congregation gave strength to those individuals forced to praise God in persecution. "When in hunger and cold, between interrogations, or as one sentenced to death, he was privileged to praise God, he knew that in all his ways he was borne up by the church's praise of God."[14]

This praise of God is not so much an attitude as it is an action. It is not a feeling but an active response to God. Joel Filártiga is a medical doctor living and working with the poorest of the poor in Paraguay. With his wife, Nidia, he runs a small clinic in Ybyqui, a town two hours' drive from the capital of Paraguay, Asuncion. Joel Filártiga is also an artist. He expresses the abandonment and despair of the poor through his art. He gives voice to their struggle for justice. In March, 1976, Filártiga's son, Joelito, was kidnapped by the police, tortured, and killed. His death did not drive them into silence and seclusion. Joel and his wife cried out in protest. "Instead of dressing their son's electroshocked, burned, and distorted body in fine clothes and making it look peaceful, they laid it naked on the bloody mattress on which it had been found." Filártiga's drawings took on a new urgency and power. He drew with pen and pencil during long nights of tears, after long and frustrating sessions with judges and lawyers. His drawings are statements of hope. Some of them have illustrated books sympathetic to the struggle for peace and justice.[15] His art is protest and praise. It is an act of defiance before powers and principalities that demand for themselves what belongs only to God.

Our praise of God, though separated by thousands of miles and immense political and cultural differences, is part of Joel Filártiga's praise. Our praise of God in the psalms bears up those who must praise God and struggle for justice in cold and hunger, in prison or awaiting execution. Our praise of God in the psalms grounds and tethers us firmly in reality. It prohibits our flight into our own timeless world of scattered images and feelings. The psalms speak to those who hunger for reality and for shalom. They satisfy those whose thirst can be quenched only in the concrete realities of history. We are all seeking the lost spoor of our meanings. Each of us longs for definition, even as we attempt to define our longings. This twin impulse achieves its fulfillment in the psalms.

Questions for Reflection/Discussion

1. Take a few minutes to read several of the following psalms in silence: Psalms 50, 78, 81, 103, and 104 through 107.

2. What do these psalms suggest about our relationship with God?

3. How do the psalms summarize our faith for us?

4. How might memorization of specific psalms or verses from the psalms enable us to better express our faith?

5. Discuss your reflections with your partner if you are comfortable doing so. You may also want to record your insights in your journal.

APPENDIX ONE: *Organization of the Psalter*[1]

THE PSALTER HAS a composite structure that leaves the reader with an initial sense of disorder. This structure was built up from various collections of psalms that scribes brought together at difference times over several hundred years.

Psalms 3 through 41 all bear a Davidic label that identifies David as their author. These seem to form a compact and uniform collection that was brought into the Psalter as a whole. Psalms 42 through 49 represent a separate collection attributed to a musical guild found within the Temple, the sons of Korah. Psalms 51 through 72 also bear a Davidic attribution. They, however, cannot be a part of the earlier Davidic psalms. Psalms 51 through 72 consistently refer to God as *Elohim*, while Psalms 3 through 41 call God *Yahweh*. This slight difference has led some scholars to classify Psalms 42 through 83 as an Elohistic Psalter. Since the northern kingdom of Israel tended to prefer *Elohim* to *Yahweh* as a divine name, this collection may have been used at an important northern shrine such as Shiloh or Bethel or Dan. Refugees who fled the northern kingdom when it was overrun by Assyria in 722 B.C. may have brought this Elohistic Psalter south with them. Eventually someone incorporated it into the Temple collection.

Psalms 50 and 73 through 83 represent another separate collection. These psalms are attributed to another guild of Temple musicians, the sons of Asaph. Psalms 84 through 89 seem to form an appendix to this portion of the Psalter. Presumably an early collection ended at Psalm 83 and other psalms attributed to a variety of Temple guilds were appended in 84 through 89.

With Psalm 90 we seem to encounter the beginning of

another large division in the Psalter. Psalms 90 through 150 can be divided into four separate collections. Only Psalms 119 and 137 do not fit into this scheme. Probably they were added at a much later date, and therefore did not fit into the original plan. Psalms 90 through 104 are distinguished by the fact that the majority of these are songs of "access to the divine throne." Sometimes these psalms are called enthronement psalms because of their refrain, "Yahweh is king." Psalms 104 through 106 form a conclusion to this collection. These psalms represent the first block of Hallel psalms. Their label, *Hallel*, arises from their call to praise God. A small block of such Hallel psalms seems to conclude each of the four divisions within Psalms 90 through 150.

Psalms 108 through 110 are another small collection to which David's name is attached. Psalms 111 through 118 represent the second block of Hallel psalms. Following these one finds a collection of songs of pilgrimage or songs of ascent in Psalms 120 through 134. A third block of Hallel psalms, Psalms 135 through 136, concludes this division. Psalms 139 through 145 are still another Davidic collection, and they end with the Hallel psalms of 146 through 150.

Psalms 137 and 119 do not fit well into this scheme. Consequently, some scholars theorize that a scribe who valued them and feared that they might be lost added them to the established collection sometime later in the Psalter's evolution. Psalms 1 and 2 were also composed after the collection was well-established. They seem to be an introduction to the whole Psalter. Psalm 1 commends the study of the Psalter for its insight into the will of God. Psalm 2, on the other hand, exhorts the reader to understand the psalms as a testimony to the Messiah. They draw the Psalter into the orbit of the law and the prophets. This was an important step in transforming the Psalter from a collection of hymns used in the Temple into a collection of scripture upon which the faithful privately can meditate.

Superimposed over this organizational plan is another set of divisions. This scheme seeks to divide the Psalter into five books, presumably because the Torah of Moses has five books. If the addition of Psalms 1 and 2 began the process of transforming the Temple hymns into a collection of poems upon which to contemplate God's will and law, then this second organizational plan completed the process. The psalms, like the Torah, have become a divine word meant for individual rumination and edification. These divisions are still found in the text. Each ends with a brief doxology:

1. Psalms 1 through 41   Doxology: 41:13
2. Psalms 42 through 72   Doxology: 72:18–19
3. Psalms 73 through 89   Doxology: 89:52
4. Psalms 90 through 106   Doxology: 106:48
5. Psalms 107 through 149   Doxology: 150

As one can easily discern, the existing divisions do not organize the Psalter into compact and separate types of psalms. Laments, songs of trust, creation hymns, and praises of Zion and the royal monarchy are all indiscriminately intermingled. No principle of organization has gathered together all the psalms of lament into one place and the hymns to Zion in another. We must simply familiarize ourselves with the categories and collections so that we know where to turn for a specific psalm.

APPENDIX TWO: *Form for Morning and Evening Prayer*

THE MATERIAL IN this book is designed so that the chapters can be used as an eight-week study for individuals or groups.

The psalms formed the basis for the monastic rhythm of corporate prayer. At the time of the English Reformation, Thomas Cranmer, Archbishop of Canterbury, adapted these offices into the parish services of morning and evening prayer. These services have provided the foundation for public worship among English-speaking peoples.

I would urge each study group to begin their time together with an order of worship based upon these classic services. Individuals may also want to adapt the format into their own devotional study. The July/August 1983 issue of *alive now!*, published by The Upper Room, contains an expanded version of these liturgies and suggests several musical settings appropriate to them. The following is a condensed format.

Morning Praise

Opening
  Leader: O Lord, open our lips;
  People: And we shall declare your praise.

Hymn

Psalm
  Unison, antiphonal, or individual reading of psalm
    or psalms
  Silence
  Psalm prayer

Scripture
  Reading from the Hebrew Bible or New Testament
  Silence

Canticle of Praise
> Unison reading or singing of one of the following:
>> Song of Moses: Exodus 15:1–6, 11–13, 17–18
>> Song of Isaiah: Isaiah 55:6–11
>> Song of Zechariah: Luke 1:68–79
>> Song of Mary: Luke 1:46–55
>> Song of Simeon: Luke 2:29–32
>> Song of the Redeemed: Revelation 15:3–4
>> Gloria in Excelsis
>> Te Deum Laudamus

Prayers of Petition, Intercession, and Thanksgiving

The Lord's Prayer

Dismissal
> Leader: May Jesus Christ, who has come for our salvation and who is coming again in glory, guide and protect us this day.
> People: Amen.

Evening Praise

Opening
> Leader: Light and peace in Jesus Christ;
> People: Thanks be to God.

Hymn

Psalm
> Unison, antiphonal, or individual reading of psalm or psalms
> Silence
> Psalm prayer

Scripture
> Reading from the Hebrew Bible or New Testament
> Silence

Canticle of Praise
> Unison reading or singing of one of the following:
>> Song of Moses: Exodus 15:1–6, 11–13, 17–18
>> Song of Isaiah: Isaiah 55:6–11
>> Song of Zechariah: Luke 1:68–79

Song of Mary: Luke 1:46–55
Song of Simeon: Luke 2:29–32
Gloria in Excelsis
Te Deum Laudamus

Prayers of Petition, Intercession, and Thanksgiving

The Lord's Prayer

Dismissal
Leader: Eternal Creator of light, yours is the morning and yours is the evening. Draw us to yourself so there will be no darkness within us.
People: Amen.

NOTES

Chapter One

1. Laurens Van Der Post, *The Lost World of the Kalahari* (New York: Pyramid Publications, 1966), p. 66.
2. Max Weber, *The Protestant Ethic and the Spirit of Capitalism* (New York: Charles Scribner's Sons, 1930), p. 182.

Chapter Two

1. Brevard S. Childs, *Introduction to the Old Testament as Scripture* (Philadelphia: Fortress Press, 1979), p. 521.
2. Childs, *Introduction to the Old Testament*, p. 521.
3. Claus Westermann, *Praise and Lament in the Psalms*, trans. Keith R. Crim and Richard N. Soulen (Atlanta: John Knox Press, 1981), p. 275.
4. George E. Mendenhall, *The Tenth Generation* (Baltimore: Johns Hopkins University Press, 1973), pp. 90-95.
5. Edward Schillebeeckx, *Jesus*, trans. Hubert Hoskins (New York: Vintage Books, 1981), p. 638.
6. Meister Eckart, *Breakthrough* (Garden City, N.Y.: Image Books, 1980), p. 217.
7. Westermann, *Praise and Lament in the Psalms*, p. 162.

Chapter Three

1. Lillian Hellman, *Pentimento* (New York: Signet, 1973), p. 1.
2. Walter Brueggemann, *Praying the Psalms* (Winona, Minn.: St. Mary's Press, 1982), p. 17.
3. Brueggemann, *Praying the Psalms*, p. 44.
4. *Seasons of the Gospel* (Nashville: Abingdon, 1979), p. 106.

Chapter Four

1. Alfred North Whitehead, *Process and Reality*, ed. David Ray Griffin and Donald W. Sherburne, (New York: Free Press, 1978), p. 346.

Chapter Five

1. John Macquarrie, *Principles of Christian Theology* (New York: Charles Scribner's Sons, 1966), p. 306.
2. Annie Dillard, *Pilgrim at Tinker Creek* (New York: Harper's Magazine Press, 1974), pp. 78-79.
3. Thomas Merton, *New Seeds of Contemplation* (New York: New Directions, 1972), pp. 34-35.
4. Fritjof Capra, *The Tao of Physics* (Berkeley: Shambala, 1975), p. 23.
5. Capra, *The Tao of Physics*, p. 23.
6. Erik Erikson, *Insight and Responsibility* (New York: Norton, 1964), p. 105.
7. Loren Eiseley, *The Unexpected Universe* (New York: Harcourt, Brace, World 1969), p. 182.
8. Eiseley, *The Unexpected Universe*, p. 230.
9. Thomas Merton, *Zen and the Birds of Appetite* (New York: New Directions, 1968), p. 55.
10. Merton, *Zen and the Birds of Appetite*, p. 56.
11. Bernard Lonergan, *Method in Theology* (New York: Herder and Herder, 1972), pp. 6-9.
12. Eckhart, *Breakthrough*, pp. 216-217.
13. Carol Murphy, *The Valley of the Shadow*, Pendle Hill Pamphlet 184, p. 10.
14. Paul Reps, comp., *Zen Flesh, Zen Bones* (Anchor Books, n.d.), p. 5.
15. St. John of the Cross, *Ascent of Mount Carmel*, trans. E. Allison Peers (Garden City, N.Y.: Image Books, 1958), pp. 156-157.

Chapter Six

1. Paul Tillich, *On the Boundary* (New York: Charles Scribner's Sons, 1966), p. 97.
2. David Tracy, *Blessed Rage for Order* (New York: Seabury, 1975), p. 108.
3. Johannes B. Metz, *Poverty of Spirit*, trans. John Drury (Paramus, NJ: Paulist Press, 1968), p. 18.
4. Eckhart, *Breakthrough*, pp. 216-217.
5. Brueggemann, *Praying the Psalms*, p. 28.
6. Brueggemann, *Praying the Psalms*, p. 40.
7. Athanasius, *The Life of Anthony and the Letter to Marcellinus*, trans. Robert C. Gregg (New York: Paulist Press, 1980), p. 109.

Chapter Seven

1. T. S. Eliot, "Little Gidding," *The Complete Poems and Plays, 1909-1950* (New York: Harcourt, Brace, and World, Inc., 1971), pp. 138-139.
2. A. L. Maycock, *Nicholas Ferrar of Little Gidding* (Grand Rapids, Mich.: Eerdmans Publishing Co., 1980), pp. 202-219.
3. Dietrich Bonhoeffer, *Prisoner for God: Letters and Papers from Prison* (New York: The Macmillan Co., 1953), p. 32.
4. Westermann, *Praise and Lament in the Psalms*, p. 5.
5. Dietrich Bonhoeffer, *Psalms: The Prayer Book of the Bible,* trans., James H. Burtness (Minneapolis: Augsburg Publishing House, 1974), p. 26.
6. Lawrence Cunningham, *Saint Francis of Assisi* (San Francisco: Harper and Row, Publishers, 1981), pp. 36-37.
7. Samuel Terrien, *The Psalms and Their Meaning for Today* (Indianapolis: The Bobbs-Merrill Co., Inc., 1952), p. ix.
8. Childs, *Introduction to the Old Testament*, p. 523.
9. Edmund Fuller, ed., *The Showing Forth of Christ: Sermons of John Donne* (New York: Harper and Row, Publishers, 1964), p. 125.
10. St. Teresa of Avila, *The Life of Teresa and Jesus*, trans., E. Allison Peers (Garden City, NY: Image Books, 1960), p. 185.
11. Massey H. Shepherd Jr., *The Psalms in Christian Worship* (Minneapolis: Augsburg Publishing House, 1976), pp. 40-41.

Chapter Eight

1. Gabe Huck, *Liturgy Needs Community Needs Liturgy* (New York: Paulist, 1973), pp. 45-50.
2. Wallace Stevens, "The Motive For Metaphor," *Collected Poems* (New York: Alfred K. Knopf, 1969), p. 288.
3. C. S. Lewis, *Reflections on the Psalms* (New York: Harcourt Brace, 1958), pp. 58-59.
4. Eiseley, *The Unexpected Universe*, pp. 145-46.
5. Bonhoeffer, *Psalms: The Prayer Book of the Bible*, p. 26.
6. Northrop Frye, *The Educated Imagination* (Bloomington, Ind.: Indiana Univ. Press, 1971), p. 121.
7. Athanasius, *Letter to Marcellinus*, p. 124.
8. Terrien, *The Psalms and Their Meaning for Today,* pp. 269-70.
9. Lewis, *Reflections on the Psalms*, p. 93.
10. Lewis, *Reflections on the Psalms*, pp. 94-97.
11. Westermann, *Praise and Lament in the Psalms*, p. 159.
12. John Milton, *Paradise Lost* (New York: Airmont, Inc., 1968), p. 179.

13. Westermann, *Praise and Lament in the Psalms*, p. 161.

14. Westermann, *Praise and Lament in the Psalms*, p. 6.

15. Donald P. McNeill, Douglas A. Morrison, Henri J. M. Nouwen, *Compassion* (Garden City, NY: Doubleday, 1982), pp. 141-142.

Appendix One

1. Bernhard W. Anderson, *Out of the Depths* (Philadelphia: Westminster, 1964).

About the Author

Thomas R. Hawkins, pastor of Northside United Methodist Church in South Dennis, Massachusetts, received the B.A. degree from Eastern Illinois University, the M.A. degree from Indiana University and from Harvard University, and the M. Div. degree from Christian Theological Seminary in Indianapolis.

In addition to serving pastorates in Massachusetts and Indiana, Mr. Hawkins also served as coordinator for the Southern New England Conference Council on Youth Ministry for two years. He is actively involved in the Southern New England Emmaus Movement and has been a participant in The Upper Room's Academy for Spiritual Formation.

In discussing *The Unsuspected Power of the Psalms,* Mr. Hawkins explains, "Through the psalms we hear the great chorus of the people of God who responded and are responding continually to God's presence and absence in their lives. The psalms catch us up in this same story and remind us that it is our story, our hymn of praise."

Mr. Hawkins, an amateur potter, also finds time to play the flute.